CW00661328

STOP STRESS EATING NOW

HOW TO OVERCOME EMOTIONAL EATING FAST

JOHN BENSON

CONTENTS

THANK YOU

Thank you for purchasing this book, this means a lot to a self publish author like me.

As gesture of gratitude, please grab a free copy of my "Change your habits and these will change you".

Click >here< or scan the barcode below!

Let me know what you think!

John

INTRODUCTION

"I am forever engaged in a silent battle in my head over whether or not to lift the fork to my mouth." — Jena Morrow

After a long day at the office, do you ever just want to relax with some cheesecake or a packet of chips? If this is the case, you are not alone. Stressful situations engage systems related to metabolism, thinking, and rewards.

According to research, people who experience high chronic stress levels are more likely to indulge in stress eating. Some people react to stress not only emotionally but also physically. A stressful situation causes the body to generate cortisol, the hormone which aids in self-defense. When cortisol levels remain high for an extended period, as they often do in response to chronic stress, the body adapts by eating more, storing more fat, and gaining weight.

For stress eaters, the primary motivation for eating isn't to satisfy hunger but rather to alleviate feelings of sadness, loneliness, boredom, anger, etc. Unfortunately, stress eating is not a solution to emotional difficulties; it frequently worsens your mood. Once you've binged on food to cope with your emotions, you're still left with the initial problem and the guilt associated with your behavior.

It's not necessarily a terrible thing to sometimes use food as a mood booster, reward, or celebration. But, if reaching for food whenever you are feeling down, angry, depressed, lonely, tired, or restless is your go-to method to deal with these emotions, you will likely get trapped in an unpleasant rut. You will never address the underlying feelings or issues causing the stress eating.

You can't eat your way out of emotional hunger.

Eating might seem nice at the time, but the sentiments that prompted the eating remain. Not only do you take in extra calories, but you will most likely feel worse after eating. You punish yourself mentally for failing to exercise more self-control and making mistakes.

You feel increasingly helpless over your eating habits and emotions, which compounds the issue of not learning more effective methods of dealing with your emotions. No matter how helpless you feel about your eating habits and how you feel, you can always change for the better.

Using the guidelines covered in this book, you can cut down on stress eating, win the battle against cravings, pinpoint the causes of your binges, and replace them with healthier coping mechanisms.

What are my thoughts on food and emotional eating?

I could always turn to food for solace whenever I was feeling down. One of the best ways to bond with people and make lasting memories is by sharing a meal together. I've always had a passion for exploring various foods.

Our culture puts a premium on outward looks, and it's easy to become caught up in constant comparisons to others. Negative self-talk about my appearance and a general sense of not being good enough are constant battles for me.

Knowing that our identities are comprised of more than how we interact with food can be empowering. In reality, there is much more to us than what meets the eye. One way to care for ourselves is by feeding our bodies nutritious and tasty meals.

Through this inquiry, I hope you'll view food for what it really is: a source of life-sustaining energy and delicious satisfaction and come to value your special bond with it.

1

WHAT IS STRESS EATING?

"When I am in trouble, eating is the only thing that consoles me. Indeed, when I am in really great trouble, as anyone who knows me intimately will tell you, I refuse everything except food and drink. At the present moment, I am eating muffins because I am unhappy. Besides, I am particularly fond of muffins." — Oscar Wilde.

When was the last time you numbed your feelings with food?

Many people can relate to this feeling. You had a stressful day at work, maybe you fought with one of your coworkers, or your boss criticized you in front of everyone. You go home, order a large pizza and eat it by yourself and have a box of donuts for dessert. Sounds familiar? Do you find food therapeutic? Do you turn to food for comfort when stressed about work, your relationship, or exams? If you answer yes, you rely on food to escape your issues which can be a problem.

However, for every problem, there is a solution. This chapter introduces the concept of stress eating, the reasons behind it, its triggers, and its effects on your mental and physical health.

Stress Eating Explained

Food can bring comfort. Having burgers and fries for dinner after a long day at work or running around after the kids can be very relaxing and satisfying. However, if you turn to food whenever you feel stressed or upset, this is a problem. You aren't just giving yourself a treat at the end of a hard day; you are using food as a coping mechanism. This is referred to as stress eating.

As it is clear from the name, stress or emotional eating is when a person deals with negative emotions or stressful situations by overeating. This behavior isn't related to hunger. It is usually an emotional response, like the saying, "you eat your feelings." In other words, you eat because you believe food will make you feel better or remove your stress, which isn't true. The stress might not only be emotional, but it is also mental or physical.

If food is the answer to your problems, don't worry, you aren't alone; we have all been there. The American Psychological Association conducted a survey in 2015 that showed two in five American adults use eating as a coping mechanism. With recent events happening in the world, we expect the number to be much higher. About 75% of the time, we eat because we are stressed or bored rather than hungry. Women are known to use food as a coping mechanism more than men; it is one of the reasons behind obesity in women.

When you observe your eating patterns, you will realize that hunger isn't the only motive behind eating. Since the popularity of streaming services like Netflix, people find it relaxing to mindlessly eat comfort food while watching their favorite TV show and forgetting about the world. You might think: what is wrong with turning to food for comfort? The problem with stress eating is it is unhealthy behavior. People don't eat an apple or a salad when they are stressed, they resort to junk food like pizza, fries, burgers, pies, ice cream, etc. Food won't make you feel any better or satisfy your emotional needs, and you will also gain weight and inherit other health issues.

There is no harm in eating a large meal to celebrate an occasion or treat yourself once in a while. However, if you're dealing with stress by eating rather than other healthy behaviors like exercising, talking to a friend, or journaling, you are a victim of stress eating. You fail to address the problem and create more issues by eating your feelings. Stress eating also makes you feel worse, as guilt usually occurs after overeating. It is a vicious cycle: you get upset, you overeat, you feel guilty, and you overeat again.

When you use eating as a coping mechanism, you deprive yourself of adopting healthy behavior to provide solutions rather than adding to your problem. Food becomes a comfort zone, something you turn to without even thinking. You will feel powerless over food and weak in confronting your feelings.

Emotional Hunger vs. Physical Hunger

You might not be aware you are stress-eating and believe you're eating habits are normal. It is significant to differentiate between physical and emotional hunger. Stress eaters struggle to tell the difference as they have become accustomed to dealing with their emotions by eating. You feel a strong emotional hunger when you are upset, sad, angry, or stressed. Naturally, you confuse it with regular hunger.

Stress eating is a mindless act; you won't notice how it affects you until you try on your favorite outfit, and it doesn't fit. Think of the last time you tried on an old outfit and realized it didn't fit. Trust me; this can be the breaking point that will make you evaluate your eating habits.

Distinguishing between both types of hunger will help you battle stress eating. Emotional hunger, unlike regular hunger, isn't a physical feeling like a growling in your stomach. It feels like a powerful craving you can't fight. With regular hunger, you eat anything to satisfy this feeling, but with emotional hunger, you have a specific food in mind; it is often sweets or junk food. You can taste it in your mouth, and nothing else will fill this "hunger."

Regular hunger is a gradual feeling. You don't suddenly become starving. It isn't the case with emotional hunger, which is an urgent overwhelming feeling that must be satisfied right away. However, satisfying this urge often results in various negative emotions like guilt and regret. Eating shouldn't make you feel guilty as you supply your body with the nutrients to stay healthy and active.

Nothing can ever satisfy this hunger, no matter how much you eat, unlike regular hunger, when you feel full after you eat. There is a void inside of you, and you are trying to fill it with food. The only result is you overeat, feel bloated, and uncomfortable while still feeling stressed. You will be surprised at how much food you eat when you finish eating.

Stress eating is based on an emotional response, so you often mindlessly eat because it isn't real hunger. Regular hunger makes you more aware of your portions, and you stop eating when you feel full.

With emotional hunger, food is only a distraction, like watching TV or playing a game on your phone. It's meant to create a barrier between you and your emotions. Instead of confronting them, you distract yourself by eating.

Reasons behind Stress Eating

We all have friends or family with healthy habits when dealing with stress. They don't grab a box of donuts each time they fight with their partner or eat a large pizza when-ever they have a bad day. They go for a run, talk out their emotions, or write in their diary. Food provides sustenance, not comfort.

It is unrealistic to handle bad days and every inconvenience by eating. Sometimes, our bad days can last for weeks or even months. For instance, if you work in a stressful envi-ronment, you might overeat every day to escape the pres-sure of your job. It will be very harmful to your health and weight.

There is a reason some people stress eat while others don't. The good news is it isn't our fault. It is our hormones. According to dietitian Allison Knott, when you suffer from stress, the cortisol hormone levels rise, increasing your appetite, and you feel hungry. Cortisol also makes you crave unhealthy, fatty, or sugary food. If you have chronic stress, this hormone will always be high, leading you to feel real hunger that can only be satisfied by junk food filled with carbohydrates.

Food brings us joy. Think of how you feel when you eat your favorite dish or have the first bite of your favorite pizza. Our brains react to food similarly to drugs, although not to the same degree. Foods like sugar or carbohydrates are responsible for releasing dopamine, a chemical that makes us feel pleasure, similar to drugs like cocaine. Sugary food also contributes to the release of endogenous opioids, which cause a pleasant feeling.

Compulsive eating is similar to alcohol and drugs. They make us feel good for a short time but much worse afterward. It's like taking a painkiller for chronic pain rather than seeing a doctor to find a cure.

There has always been a stigma around mental health, and that is why many have learned to shove down our emotions. Some people regard feelings of sadness or anger as weakness. Many would rather stay at home, eating their feelings away, than reach out and ask for help. Luckily, we live in a day and age where people are more educated about mental health, and opening up about our feelings is encouraged.

We have been taught that food is an effective mood booster. Movies always show people going through an emotional crisis sitting on their couch and eating from a bucket of ice cream. Marketing agencies also take advantage of this idea with ads promoting the notion that food will make you feel better. For instance, chocolate ads show someone having a bad day but eating one bite of chocolate turned their day around. As a result, we have been programmed to reach out for food because we believe it can make us feel better.

There is always food in our homes. You have snacks in your fridge, ingredients in your kitchen to cook your favorite dish, or you can simply order from your favorite restaurant. Food is easily accessible to many, making stress eating more convenient.

The COVID-19 pandemic also led many people to stress eating and why we gained weight during the quarantine. We were sitting at home in a closed environment and following the news of people dying and getting sick. It was a very stressful situation for everyone, and food was one of the few things that provided distraction and comfort.

The Impact of Stress Eating on Your Health

You might think stress eating will only make you gain weight. However, it is an unhealthy habit that negatively impacts your mental and physical health.

Weight Gain

Weight gain is obvious but is still worth mentioning. When stress eating becomes a behavioral pattern, it leads to weight gain. You are mindlessly eating, so you don't watch your food intake, which has serious consequences, like obesity. Weight gain leads to various health problems like constant fatigue, diabetes, and high blood pressure.

However, eating healthy food when stressed will not prevent weight gain. The high cortisol level in your body slows down your metabolism, making losing weight difficult.

Guilt

After you overeat, you have a moment of clarity and realize you ate more than you should have. It is when you feel guilty, especially if you watch your weight and this behavior is ruining your diet. Guilt makes your mood and stress even worse. What do you do when you feel more stressed? You stress eat again. It's a vicious circle. Guilt leads to other issues like low self-esteem. Ultimately, you start hating yourself for not handling your stress healthily.

Heartburn

Your body doesn't digest food easily when stressed. Your stomach releases an acid to speed up the process. Consequently, when you stress eat, you get indigestion and heartburn. When you have chronic stress, your body constantly releases stomach acid at high levels. This stomach acid causes other health problems like GERD.

Immune System

You eat healthily, but if you are constantly stressed, the high cortisol levels prevent the body from working efficiently and absorbing nutrients like iron, zinc, magnesium, and calcium. It weakens your immune system and will not have what it takes to fight infections. Remember, your immune system acts as a shield protecting your body from diseases. Providing it with nutrients will be useless if the stress prevents your immune system from using them.

Nausea

When we overeat, our stomachs and body cannot handle large amounts of food, so nausea is a common symptom of overeating. If you have chronic stress and deal with it by stress eating, you will often feel nauseated.

Digestion Issues

Your body releases cortisol as a reaction to stress. It prepares us to handle the situation. Cortisol focuses on the body functions that keep you alert. The sugar levels in your blood rise to give the brain more energy. Other functions are left unattended since they will not be much help in a fight-or-flight situation. One of these functions is your digestive system. As most of your blood goes to your other functions, it does not leave much blood for the digestive process, and the food in your body will not be digested properly. Stress eating negatively impacts your digestion, making you feel bloated and nauseous.

Digestive issues can have serious consequences. If you have chronic stress, it can damage your digestive system and cause diseases like gastroesophageal reflux disease and irritable bowel syndrome.

Causes and Triggers

Now that you know the impact of stress eating on your physical health, you probably wonder how to avoid this unhealthy habit. The first thing to do is identify your triggers. Everyone is triggered by something that makes us eat mindlessly. Recognizing the most common stress-eating triggers can help to avoid them or become aware that your hunger isn't physical but emotional.

Anxiety

One of the main triggers behind stress eating is anxiety. Anxiety makes us confused, worried, and constantly on edge. Food presents comfort, albeit temporary, but people believe it will ease their anxiety. Think of the last time you were anxious. How did you handle the situation? You probably grabbed all the junk food around the house and ate while watching Netflix. Don't feel bad. Many of us deal with our anxiety the same way. However, if anxiety triggers you to stress eat, you must look for healthier coping mechanisms to help you deal with your emotions.

However, some people lose their appetite when anxious as they become overwhelmed with their emotions, and food is usually the last thing on their minds.

Winter Blues

Some people feel stressed during winter. The days are shorter, the weather is cold, and the holidays can be stressful. Many feel stressed just thinking of family gatherings during the holidays. Also, different foods are consumed during these occasions, making it convenient to reach out and grab your favorite snack to escape your emotions.

Diet

There is nothing wrong with eating junk food now and then. However, some people are so obsessed with staying in shape that they go on strict diets. Dieting usually focuses on healthy food, eliminating unhealthy ones. But these restrictions can lead to emotional eating. If you deprive yourself of a certain food, you will always crave it and eat it in large quantities, leading to weight gain and the vicious cycle we discussed earlier. Severe diets also put you in a bad mood or frustrate and stress you, which also leads to emotional eating.

Stressful Situations

Some situations are so stressful that you cope by eating rather than dealing with them directly. These situations depend on the person. It could be your job, partner, family, or even watching the news. Recognizing the situations that trigger your emotional eating is necessary to overcome this bad habit.

Numbing the Emotions

We stress eat to escape or numb our emotions. Food offers a distraction from loneliness, sadness, anger, shame, anxiety, or fear. Deep down, we know food isn't a solution, but we keep eating because food provides comfort and an escape from these negative emotions for a very short while.

Trauma

Traumatic experiences make life hard. Sometimes, you cannot sit alone with your thoughts as the pain and negativity can be too much to handle. Your thoughts are stuck in the past, living with the painful memories or struggling with the triggers. It makes it hard for you to live in the moment or focus on the future. You always look for an escape from the memories you can neither live with nor change. With so much negativity going on, you direct your thoughts to something positive and more gratifying, food.

Victims of violence or rape look for ways to exert control over their lives since these incidents were beyond their control yet changed their lives forever. Food gives them control and turns them into victims and abusers. Overeating is how they abuse their bodies, and their inability to stop eating is how they become victims of the abuse. Food becomes many things, a distraction and a tool to soothe the pain, and helps them feel more in control over their lives.

Pregnancy

You have probably heard a pregnant woman saying, "I have to eat. I am eating for two." While pregnant women eat more than usual and often have cravings, stress eating is different. You eat even when you aren't hungry, and you cannot control your eating habits. You only stop eating when you get sick, but even this doesn't stop you from overeating when you feel better.

Usually, women who stress eat before pregnancy follow the same pattern during pregnancy. Overeating affects your health and your baby's, too. Your doctor will struggle to monitor your child's development due to your weight gain, which can lead to high blood pressure, long labor, premature birth, and miscarriage.

Filling the Void

Some negative emotions make us feel empty inside. It feels as if food is the best way to fill this void because of the pleasure it gives us, even if it is for a few minutes. Sometimes this emptiness results from an unfulfilled life. Maybe you can't find a job, have money troubles, or fail to achieve a big dream. You don't want to think about your failures or what went wrong, so you distract yourself with food instead. The promise of a good meal can be the only thing that gets you through the day.

Some people also confuse hunger with boredom. When you don't have anything to do, eating becomes a habit you turn to whenever you are bored.

Everything in life is better and healthier in moderation. Overeating has serious consequences on your health and life. You cannot confront your issues or solve problems if you keep eating rather than dealing with them. Stress eating will leave you with more issues to worry about than you began with. You deprive yourself of the chance to learn healthy coping mechanisms to provide you with real solutions. Remember, food only makes you feel better for a couple of hours but makes you feel worse for days.

Stress eating is a bad habit that can feel out of control sometimes. However, I want to tell you that it is possible to get rid of it for good. It will take time and effort, but you are on your way. You have taken the first step, and there is still more to come.

Key Takeaways

- Understanding what stress eating is
- The difference between physical and emotional eating
- How stress eating affects your mental and physical health
- Triggers of stress eating
- Food is only a temporary solution and can't fix your problems
- Stress eating is caused by hormones
- You can't eat your emotions away

Now that you have become well-informed about stress eating, we invite you to go to the next chapter and learn where stress eating starts.

2

WHERE STRESS EATING STARTS

"*E*motions can powerfully affect food cravings. For many people who struggle with food addiction, stress eating, or emotionally eat; please know that food cravings are often not about physical hunger. Our "thinking mind" has very little control over our emotions and food craving." - Dr. Kirsten Grant

This dedicated chapter discusses the different causes of stress eating. You must first uncover where this behavior begins to deal with stress eating efficiently. As you will learn, stress eating has several components, including psychological and physiological. From hormones to social situations, the origins of this behavior can stem from the most unlikely places. More importantly, each cause affects your relationships with food in different stages of life. The chapter delves into different situations you might face in childhood, adulthood, or adolescence, which lead to stress eating.

Stress and Hormones

From a physiological standpoint, stress and eating are regulated by specific metabolic activities, or the lack thereof. When the body or mind experiences stress, they signal the brain to release hormones to help you deal with the symptoms of anxiety and stress.

Adrenaline and Cortisol

Your body's first response to stress is to release adrenaline and noradrenaline in the sympathetic nervous system. These two hormones are responsible for the "fight-or-flight" response. Then, your hypothalamic-pituitary-adrenal (HPA) axis is activated, starting with the release of adrenocorticotropic hormone (ACTH) and cortisol from the pituitary gland. The latter is directly related to appetite control in stressful times.

In acute stress, the nervous system inhibits the appetite, sending out adrenaline, which shuts down hunger cues. It acts as a survival mechanism, so your body and mind can focus on resolving the situation - or getting away from it. So, when you are suddenly faced with a stressful situation, you won't feel hungry even when you're supposed to be. Your appetite will be suppressed because you're too busy responding to the "threat" you perceive.

However, if the stress and anxiety become chronic, your body will release more cortisol than adrenaline. Cortisol promotes hunger cues, increasing your appetite and motivating you to satisfy your body's need for food. Even if the stress subsides, your body will continue to produce large amounts of cortisol if the brain doesn't register that it needs to stop the stress response. It usually happens when a person cannot process stressful events appropriately. In this fast-paced world, everyone is expected to rebound from whatever caused their stress and continue with life as if nothing happened.

The continued release of cortisol triggers the need for a coping mechanism. When you satisfy your hunger (caused by the faulty appetite control mechanism), your body registers this as the ideal way to cope. Soon, every time your cortisol levels rise, your body's response makes you crave food. And not just any food. Cortisol responds best to hyper-palatable foods (high in fat, sugar, and salt). The more anxiety you experience, the more likely you'll use these foods for stress relief.

Ghrelin

Ghrelin is a hormone directly responsible for your appetite. It suppresses cravings by controlling hunger cues. As your energy and blood glucose levels get depleted, the levels of ghrelin rise, causing your hunger and craving for food. Since your body instinctively knows that carbs represent the fastest energy source, you'll crave sugary food. Under normal circumstances, when you crave food your body doesn't need, you would stop yourself from grabbing it. Since ghrelin levels remain low, your mind knows you're not actually hungry. However, when you're stressed, your ghrelin levels are elevated even when you don't need food to restore your reserves.

Leptin

If the effects of stress on ghrelin alone wouldn't cause stress eating, its impact on leptin, the hormone that inhibits the production of ghrelin, certainly will. When you're anxious, your leptin levels are reduced due to the inflammatory reaction that follows the stress. During this process, proteins called cytokines are released into the blood. These proteins have a similar structure to leptin and can easily cover the leptin receptors. Due to this, leptin can't be activated, and the ghrelin levels will rise, causing you to be hungry when you are not.

Dopamine

Dopamine is another hormone with a tremendous role in food becoming a coping mechanism. Many of the mind's responses are learned patterns developed within a reward system. If you respond to a stimulus that results in a reward, it activates the brain's pleasure centers releasing the dopamine hormone. Dopamine is one of the "feel good" hormones your body releases as a reward for specific behavior. Eating your favorite food causes the release of dopamine, giving you positive emotions regardless of how you felt before your meal.

Unfortunately, the effects of dopamine are short-lived, and soon after they're gone, the negative feelings will return. It causes you to reach for the coping mechanism again, and when you do, you'll be rewarded with another short burst of dopamine. This mechanism is called dopamine addiction and works very similarly to other addictive behaviors, from being addicted to your phone to alcohol and drug addictions. It is as easy to become addicted to sugary, fatty, and salty food as it is to any unhealthy behavior that serves as a coping mechanism.

Stuffing Emotions

Eating is a common way to temporarily put uncomfortable emotions to the back of your mind. Whether you're stressed, angry, lonely, fearful, resentful, or sad, it all goes away when you indulge in comfort food. You're numbing them with food to avoid interacting with the emotions you don't want to feel. This action has physiological and psychological components. The physiological aspect can be traced back to the hormone cortisol and how its high levels lead to frequent hunger signals, meaning you feel hungry when you want to avoid a feeling. The psychological component acts similarly to other unhealthy behaviors, including alcohol and narcotics. It is a distraction or something you put between yourself and the uncomfortable feeling you're experiencing.

The Need to Put Emotions Aside

Unfortunately, due to busy lifestyles, and social and professional expectations, many people are forced to put their emotions aside. Negative emotions are a distraction, and they hinder productivity. You probably heard that worrying about something is a waste of time. However, it isn't always that simple. Sometimes a healthy amount of worry can make you more self-aware, allowing you to find the solution. Despite this, society often tells people that having negative emotions is a bad thing. It is particularly true for people in good financial standing, who are supposed to have "nothing to complain about." People use comfort food to help them put these feelings aside to comply with these norms and avoid dealing with emotions they aren't supposed to have. Consequently, they'll develop unhealthy eating patterns, like eating, to cope with negative emotions.

Inability to Deal with Emotions

Stuffing emotions to the back of your consciousness by occupying your mind is caused by your inability to deal with these feelings. Some people can't understand, describe or process their emotions. It is called alexithymia, a condition closely tied to emotional dysregulation or the inability to manage feelings. A third issue that might hinder your ability to deal with emotions like stress is the lack of introspective awareness. You don't realize you're stressed - but you self-medicate with food anyway.

Boredom

It might come as a surprise, but boredom can also cause stress. When you don't have anything to do, you become filled with nervous energy, and sometimes the only way to expel it is by eating. While digestion causes you to spend some pent-up energy, eating food will only create more, causing a vicious cycle. You also know eating your favorite food will take some time, so your mind won't be bored, at least for the time being. However, this only lasts for a short period, and you become bored again, and the cycle continues.

Feelings of Emptiness

Sometimes boredom is more a result of feeling emptiness and not physical or mental inactivity. This emptiness can stem from feeling unfulfilled in any area of your life. Not having the career or the lifestyle you wanted and not finding love and happiness can cause you to feel like you're missing something. Preparing and eating food gives you a purpose and temporarily distracts you from how stuck you feel in life. However, like the distraction from boredom, eating food will only mask the void for a short period. Afterward, it will be even more intensive, causing more stress and unhealthy eating habits.

Childhood Habits

Children are often rewarded for good behavior with food. If this reward is absent, the children become anxious. However, if the reward is received soon after, it causes their minds to accept food as a natural stress reliever. The same happens when children are offered ice cream and other comfort food when sick. These ingrained patterns are carried into adulthood, causing you to reach for food whenever stressed. Sometimes children form memories when eating a specific food with their parents or others close to them. If you have a favorite comfort food for stress relief, you could associate it with a fond memory.

Habits Developed in Adolescence

For many, the teenage years are about testing boundaries (theirs and other people's) and experimenting with different activities to find their path in life. Unfortunately, during these years, many long-term food-related behaviors are developed. Most behaviors come from social cues and learning what others do around us. If a teen sees their friends indulging in good food, they certainly don't want to deny themselves the same experience.

On the other hand, some food-related behaviors developed in adolescence stem from traumatic or stressful experiences. Teens have incredibly sensitive hormonal and metabolic balances disturbed by minor stressors. Bullying, seemingly unattainable expectations from parents and themselves, and the inability to manage their emotions can drive teenagers into unhealthy coping mechanisms. Food is one of the most available resources people (including teens) use to calm themselves. So, it's easy to see why many turn to comfort eating to shun the negative emotions brought on by the different stressors in life.

Unrealistic Expectations

We all have expectations in different areas of life. These are not always realistic, and false expectations greatly affect your relationship with food. Expectations in romantic relationships are often carried from one relationship to another. For example, people with dependable partners in the past will expect their current or future partners to be reliable. People who don't have reliable partners will not expect their current or future partners to be dependable either. If these expectations are not met, people turn to the only thing they can rely on to soothe them, food. Whether you have unattainable expectations of your partner or they expect something unrealistic from you, it can drive you to stress eating.

Perfectionism is another form of setting an unrealistic expectation that can cause stress eating. Perfectionists live high-strung lives to present themselves in the best way possible. They tie their self-worth to their actions and accomplishments. They have to be the perfect parent, partner, employee, friend, and neighbor; otherwise, something will go terribly wrong. However, this is nearly impossible, and reality often falls short of their expectations - other people's actions or even their own shows that no one can be perfect. For perfectionists, being confronted with reality creates much stress, which they often relieve by stress eating.

Completion and Understanding

People often expect completion or unconditional support from others in different relationships. It means they want the other person's strengths to compensate for their short-comings. For example, people who are always late expect their partners and friends always to be understanding and disregard their time boundaries. Or, a coworker expects you to cover for them anytime they have to leave the workplace unexpectedly or pick up any task they fell behind on. Being the person who is always expected to understand or pick up after someone else is stressful because the other person never realizes they're doing something wrong. It is another classic situation where people turn to food for comfort.

Social Influences

People in different cultures use different occasions to gather in large groups, friends and family who celebrate the ability to spend time together. Socializing with people you haven't encountered in a while can be the ideal distraction from your everyday preoccupations. Consequently, people eat large quantities of food on these occasions. One reason this happens is to calm your anxiety in social situations. Another reason people overindulge in food during social gatherings is seeing everyone else eating. You could also be distracted by conversation and won't notice how much you've eaten. If you have friends or family members who encourage you to eat more when you would stop naturally, rather than confronting them and saying you're full, you go along because it's much easier.

Socio-Economical Background

People with poor socio-economic backgrounds are more likely to develop unhealthy eating habits, including stress eating. They often worry about wasting food, and throwing away a tiny amount of leftovers makes them anxious. It particularly applies to nutritious food because, in the past, this was something they couldn't afford. Eating the scraps of food instead of throwing them away makes people feel better about themselves.

Everyday Worries

More often than not, everyday preoccupations cause more stress and anxiety than major events in your life. Below are the most common daily stressors that can cause stress eating.

Financial Worries

Worrying about their financial situation is the number one stressor for the majority of the adult population. With so many bills to pay, who wouldn't be worried about having enough money to cover your costs? Not to mention saving for emergencies. The worry becomes even more prominent if you are responsible for children's or other adults' well-being. People often turn to food, despite grocery expenses taking up a large part of their monthly expenses to cope.

Work Stress

Work-related stress is closely tied to financial worries. After all, the best way to secure your financial situation is to have a well-paying job and possibly one with benefits. But what if this job comes with insane work hours, enough tasks to keep you awake at night, and fear of what will happen if you can't keep up with your obligations? Or, perhaps you have a colleague or employer notoriously difficult to work with? People often turn to comfort food and consume plenty of it in their short free time in these situations.

Relationship Struggles

The second most common everyday issues stem from the different emotions people experience in their relationships. Being in a dysfunctional relationship can lead to high anxiety levels, and sometimes people can only calm down through food. It typically happens in dependent or code-pendent relationships, where the expectations are high, yet the connection can't be severed. For instance, if you live with an elderly relative who exhibits toxic behavior and is entirely dependent on you. It becomes impossible to leave your relationships behind. So, every time you have a conflict with your relative, you turn to food for comfort because you feel it's the only thing that helps.

Health Worries

Not surprisingly, worrying about health issues is another reason people stress eat. Some reasons behind this fact lie in the belief that food is a form of natural medicine. However, not all food has health benefits, and certainly not when consumed as comfort and not to nourish your body. Another reason you want to overeat when you or your loved ones face a health crisis is that food is simply available. Similarly to work, financial, or relationship-related worries, worrying about your health makes you want to reach for something constant and readily available. It's a crutch you know will always be there, regardless of the outcome.

Restrictive Diet

Having a restrictive diet history puts you in a predisposition for stress eating. If you previously had a restricted diet, it was probably to lose weight or maintain it in a healthy range. During this, your mind develops a cognitive restraint, which signals that withholding food is bad and eating it is good. Due to this, many view food as a stress relief mechanism. Eating will make you feel bad, as it did when you allowed yourself a treat on a restrictive diet.

To make matters worse, the treats often treated as a reward after achieving a goal during the restrictive phase are high-calorie foods full of unhealthy fats and fast-release carbs. Once the restrictions are lifted, the possibility of a reward will continue to encourage you to turn to these foods and activate the release of dopamine from the pleasure center.

Restricting food also raises cortisol levels, further increasing the chances of stress-inducing unhealthy eating patterns. Combined with stressful events, controlling your emotions through a coping mechanism becomes even greater. In a desperate attempt to regain control, you overeat whenever you feel even a little stressed.

The level, the timing, and the duration of the restrictive period affect your relationship with food during stressful times. Flexible restrictions allow you to regulate your appetite regardless of anxiety. Rigorous restraint is more likely to cause you to lose control over your eating when stressed. Likewise, a recent restriction will have a much more enduring impact on your ability to control your appetite, as restrictive periods had over a longer duration. On the other hand, if you dieted for a couple of weeks several years ago, it is unlikely to affect your appetite when you get stressed presently.

Sleep Deprivation

Sleep deprivation is another stressor that elevates the risk of developing an unhealthy relationship with food. Depending

on how long it lasts, lack of sleep can cause stress eating
through several mechanisms.

Metabolic Imbalances

Long-term sleep deprivation leads to metabolic imbalances
putting you at risk of conditions with faulty hunger cues.
Most metabolic processes are tied to the circadian rhythm,
which gets disrupted by lack of sleep. For a healthy circadian rhythm, you'll need to sleep during the night and be
awake during the daytime. Sleep deprivation typically
causes you to be awake during nighttime, too. Insulin resistance and type II diabetes can cause you to feel hunger
more often than your body depletes its reserves. Hyperten-
sion, arteriosclerosis, and certain cardiovascular diseases
also affect the body's ability to signal fullness and hunger
cues to your brain, making you eat more than necessary. For
children, less than ten hours of sleep is enough to cause
sleep deprivation and cause metabolic imbalance. In adults,
this equates to less than five hours of sleep regularly.

Dysregulating the HPA Axis and Other Hormone Production

Lack of sleep affects the release of hormones from the HPA
axis, including cortisol. The cortisol level in the brain is
usually elevated during the day when you're surrounded by
stress stimuli, whereas when you're asleep, your body
produces less. The less you sleep, the higher the cortisol
levels. The same happens with ghrelin levels, which show
an inverse correlation with the duration and the amount of
sleep you get. Consequently, the more sleep-deprived you
are, the less leptin you produce.

Key Takeaways

Here is a summary of what you've learned from this chapter:

- The primary reason for stress eating is found in our hormonal system. Adrenalin, noradrenalin, cortisol, ghrelin, leptin, and dopamine are significant in developing unhealthy eating habits in response to stress.
- Being uncomfortable with your emotions or the inability to understand or manage them and "stuffing" them into the back of your mind with food is another coping behavior against stress.
- Boredom and the feeling of emptiness can cause people to fill in the void with food.
- Stressful childhood influences and food-related behavior learned in early childhood often cause these patterns to continue in adulthood.
- In many cultures, social gatherings are tied to food consumption and unhealthy behavior regarding food. Food is often taught to be a stress reliever, and the human mind is easily tricked into accepting this during socialization.
- Worrying about health, relationships, financial situations, or work is another reason people turn to food for comfort.
- Those with a restrictive diet history are more likely to switch this unhealthy correlation between food and stress relief to overindulgence in hyperpalatable foods.
- Sleep deprivation is known to cause a broad range of metabolic imbalances, including those affecting

the release of cortisol and ghrelin, two key
hormones affecting hunger and emotional
regulation.

The different origins of stress eating cause it to manifest
through numerous signs and symptoms. The next chapter
delves into these signs, and you'll learn to identify whether
you are a stress eater or not, so continue reading.

3

SIGNS YOU ARE A STRESS EATER

"**F**ood can distract you from your pain, but food cannot take away your pain. In fact, overeating the wrong foods can create more pain."– Karen Salmanohn

It is hard to determine whether you are eating out of hunger, boredom, or eating in response to stress. Stress-eating is difficult to overcome and often harder to pick up on. It impacts numerous aspects of life and can be detrimental to a person's mental, physical, social, and emotional health. This chapter explores signs that you're a stress eater. You'll understand each sign, how it causes you to stress eat, and impacts your life.

Signs That You Are a Stress Eater

You Eat When Under Pressure

Many people lose their appetite when they're under pressure. However, this is often a short-term response to stress. The nervous system signals to the adrenal gland, triggering the release of adrenaline. This hormone sets a person's fight-or-flight response in motion, temporarily pausing your eating.

However, this isn't the case if the pressure persists for longer. Instead of releasing adrenaline, the adrenal glands release cortisol, a stress-related hormone. Cortisol stimulates appetite and overall motivation. This motivation can be food-related too. Cortisol levels only fall when a person's stress is alleviated.

According to Harvard Medical School, many studies show that stress impacts food choices and preferences. Individuals who often feel distressed steer towards food options with high sugar or fat content, perhaps the result of high cortisol and insulin levels in the blood.

Consuming sugar- and fat-filled food instantly yet temporarily relieves stress-related emotions and bodily responses. It creates a positive feedback loop, and your behavior (eating these foods when stressed) is rewarded (you feel better), encouraging you to form this habit.

Needless to say, eating whenever you feel stressed harms your mental, emotional, and physical health. Besides weight gain, stress-eating steers you toward unhealthy food choices, increasing your risk of developing heart disease and hindering your organs' functioning. Using food as a coping mechanism when under pressure also keeps you from implementing healthy habits that help you thrive under pressure.

You Use Food to Respond to Your Emotions

Eating in response to your emotions is called emotional eating. People commonly develop emotional eating habits if they have work, financial, health, or relationship issues. People who maintain restrictive diets or have an extensive history of dieting are likely to develop emotional eating habits.

Being an emotional eater is often caused by the inability to regulate your emotions, process and describe your emotions effectively, and inadequate introspective awareness. You don't usually think before an emotional eating episode because the longer you do it, the more habitual and automatic it becomes.

Experiencing negative emotions leads to feelings of void and emptiness, which is something food can remedy. Eating triggers, the release of dopamine in the brain, a chemical associated with instigating positive emotions.

Food is a very popular coping method because it's very easily accessible. You will find something to eat if you open your fridge, cupboard, or pantry. You'll also find plenty of food options whenever you're out. It is the center of numerous things in life. Most of our outings revolve around food. We celebrate Thanksgiving, Christmas, and other events with feasts. We cook for others as a sign of love or care. Sharing food with others is a great way to bond, making us emotionally connected to food. Additionally, unlike other soothing substances, food is legal.

People who struggle with emotional eating usually feel they lose control of certain foods. They also feel the need to eat when they experience powerful emotions or even when they aren't hungry. Emotional eaters often treat food as a reward or calming agent.

Emotional eating particularly becomes a problem if you don't have other coping methods to rely on. It can be extremely harmful because even though it provides a sense of instantaneous relief, which seems like a good solution at the time, it doesn't fix the main issue. Food doesn't help you alleviate your stress, loneliness, fatigue, or boredom. It only alleviates the symptoms.

Suppose you have a fractured bone. Taking a painkiller won't fix the fracture, but it relieves some of your pain. You keep taking painkillers and applying topical antidotes instead of going to the doctor. Soon enough, these medications will lose their efficacy because you never addressed the main issue.

For most people, emotional eating is an endless loop that triggers shame and guilt, which are essentially harder to deal with than the negative emotions they started with. It is a destructive, self-perpetuating cycle.

You Find Comfort in Food

You've probably heard of the phrase "comfort food" before. Comfort food can be anything, and each person has their own idea of comfort food. Comfort foods are usually rich in fatty acids, carbs, or sugars, meaning they can be anything, ranging from chocolate fudge, ice cream, French fries, or pizza to nuts, salmon, or tuna.

Fatty acids are so comforting because they impact the same area of the brain associated with feelings, emotions, and moods. Foods high in fatty acids, carbs, and sugars are relieving because they stimulate the reward system in the brain. These are the same systems triggered by alcohol and drug consumption.

Food provides two comfort types: physical and emotional. The caudate, hippocampus, and insula are the three areas in the brain responsible for your mood. These happen to be the same three areas activated whenever you have a food craving and are responsible for the brain's reward, pleasure, and memory systems. Even though you might not necessarily have the desired amount of control over your cravings, you can improve the situation by eating a balanced diet. Ensuring to incorporate adequate amounts of healthy fats, sugars, and carbs in your daily meals will moderate your food cravings.

As for emotional comfort, this is typically satisfied by foods you grew up eating, which trigger nostalgia or ones you shared with people you love. Emotional comfort foods are associated with great relationships and memories. Emotional eating isn't necessarily bad as long as it happens in moderation and you can control it. You should be able to comfort yourself and deal with undesirable situations without turning to food for help.

You Eat to Feel Happy

Another sign you're a stress eater is you depend on food for happiness. Do you anticipate the moment you'll go home and order a cheesy pizza or look forward to eating the ice cream that awaits you at home after a long day? Food is a basic human need that helps us stay alive. You can appreciate food while eating it but can't derive happiness from it.

People with a healthy relationship with food would normally look forward to winding off after a long day by partaking in activities they enjoy or engaging in self-care. Food is not made to make us feel happy. Many of us were brought up to associate food with happy celebrations, so we naturally think it can induce feelings in us. We believe it helps fix negative emotions, fosters better ones, relieves our pressure and stress, and rewards our efforts, persistence, and hard work.

Our brain responds positively to this dopamine fix, which further reinforces the belief that food makes us happy. However, when this temporary supply of dopamine is diminished, the negative emotions return.

Food makes us feel happy because we think of it as a reward. When we were kids, our parents told us they'd give us candy or allow us to eat junk food if we finished our chores. Therefore, many still think food is a reward for making it through a tough day or powering through a challenging project at work.

Our brains are tricked into thinking that food is an incredible reward after it experiences a surge of uplifting neurotransmitters. Sounds good enough, right? Take a moment to think about how your body actually feels about this. Was it rewarded by your high sugar levels or processed food intake? Probably not. The downsides are more than the rewards.

You Eat When You're Happy

Did you know happiness can encourage you to overeat as much as sadness does? A study published in a journal called "Appetite" revealed that people usually consume more calories when watching an uplifting movie than when watching a sad one. It was found that happy situations and emotions could be as triggering as negative ones to any addiction.

Since food is often associated with connections and celebrations, many people don't realize it can be a problem. On the contrary, social gatherings encouraged us to eat past fullness. The older aunties fill our plates when they notice we're almost finished. We tell ourselves the food is incredibly delicious and it's okay to overeat on special occasions. So, we don't realize that associating food with happiness is problematic. However, when you're sad, you're likely to be aware of how much food you're consuming, even if you're stress eating. The difference is when you're happy, eating adds to your positive emotions. You think of it as part of the experience. However, when you're sad, you feel guilty and ashamed that you overate after the temporary period of relief has died down.

When we're happy, we eat because we know it's a way to keep these positive emotions. Whenever you're in a good mood, you must know this feeling won't last forever. You never know when your day will turn upside down, it can be five minutes or two hours later. So, when you feel incredibly happy, you are unconsciously tempted to keep this happiness going and eat a treat, it makes you feel even better, and you fall into this never-ending spiral.

Eating when you're happy and sad are self-medicating effort. However, in the former case, you maintain your mental state. In the latter, you numb your feelings or change them.

You're Obsessed with Food

This sign looks different for everyone. However, a very common sign someone is obsessed with food is they're always thinking about it. Do you think about what you will have for lunch as you're gulping the last bite of your breakfast burrito? Perhaps you've eaten past fullness, but you still think about what you'll eat later.

You find yourself worrying about family or holiday gatherings for days or weeks on end because you're worried you'll overeat. You dread going on vacation, even though it's supposed to bring you peace because you won't have much control over what you eat. Food-obsessed individuals usually worry about what they'll eat for their next meal or stick to certain meal times. They save calories by eating less if they know they'll have a big meal later.

Constantly thinking about food, whether beating yourself up for eating something "bad" or thinking about future meals, distracts you from focusing on work or whatever task. Some people plan their exercise around food. They'll work out before or after it to compensate for calories or severely restrict their intake on days they won't be exercising. In short, being obsessed with food means you're always thinking about it and planning your entire life around what and when you'll eat.

Food obsession is typically triggered by restriction. Have you ever gone on a strict diet that required you to cut a significant amount of calories or eliminate a certain food group, like carbs or sugar, from your diet completely? You probably found yourself craving them intensely a few days in. Perhaps you tried to substitute these cravings with diet-friendly alternatives, but they didn't satisfy enough. In that case, you tried eating these past foods in fullness, hoping it would satiate you. When you finally cave in, you eat more of your cravings than before you decided to cut them out.

The restriction also happens unconsciously. You don't necessarily have to tell yourself that a certain food group or dish is off-limits to shy away from eating it. For instance, you feel guilty after eating it or beat yourself up for eating too much of it. Your brain associates this dish with negative emotions, so you try to avoid it. When you finally convince yourself it's fine if you have a little of it, you eat but still don't feel satiated. You go and scoop yourself two more spoons, and you go back for one more until you can't stop eating.

If you suppress your cravings rather than satisfy them immediately, you feel out of control around this food. People with a healthy relationship with food realize they can eat whatever they want whenever they want, so they don't binge-eat dishes that are "off-limits." Needless to say, food obsession hinders your overall quality of life.

You Can't Stop Eating Past Fullness

It can feel like you are never satisfied regardless of how much food you eat. Your sense of satiation is short-lived, so you keep eating to keep that feeling. Take a moment to think about what comes to mind when you read the words "intuitive eating." Honoring and recognizing your hunger cues are likely among the first few things you thought of.

It is justifiable, considering diet culture continuously proves that we can't listen to our bodies and must be in charge of it. We were all somehow convinced that if we let our bodies take the reins, we'll never stop eating. However, we never thought for a moment that our bodies are much smarter than that. Your body knows what it needs to do to keep you alive every day, and it does its job seamlessly when you're in good health. If you can't trust your body, then who can you trust?

We've been taught we can't trust ourselves, so we collec- tively decided to follow a bunch of rules meant to keep us in control. A few rules tell you only to eat when you're hungry and stop whenever you're full.

Although this makes sense, the reason you're eating past fullness has nothing to do with your ability to notice when you're satiated. Some people are out of touch with their hunger cues, and that's fine (as long as they eat every 3 to 4 hours).

You can't stop eating because you aren't honoring your hunger cues or aiming to eat consistently. Your body is smart, meaning it will do anything to stay alive. You're eating even when you're full because your body doesn't trust you'll feed it the next time it signals it's hungry.

It is very harmful because it messes up your ability to recognize when you're hungry, and your body needs food. Eating past fullness makes you feel incredibly uncomfortable, irritable, and tired. Not to mention the guilt, which is often triggered by a period of restriction (causing you to eat even when you're full), that is instigated.

You Feel Uneasy Until You Fulfill a Random Craving

Everyone has food cravings from time to time, and that's completely normal. However, if you're a stress eater, you need to eat a specific food with no reasonable explanation. When you do, you'd need to satisfy this craving right away. Otherwise, you will feel uneasy and unhappy until you do.

This happens for two reasons: your propensity to restrict or because you've developed a habit of eating that food. If you repeatedly tell yourself you can't eat a particular dish or feel guilty after consuming it, it could fuel your craving and need to fulfill it on the spot.

You instill a habit in yourself. If you're craving ice cream, this isn't necessarily because you need something sweet. Is due to eating ice cream at a certain time or in a certain situation has become a habit, eventually turning into a craving.

Suppose you're used to drinking boba tea with your friends every Saturday after you go to the gym. You've accustomed yourself you'd be drinking boba tea at that time, meaning you've been looking forward to it for a while. However, your friends tell you they have errands to run on a particular Saturday, so you go home without getting drinks. You feel irritable for the rest of the day because you're craving boba tea. This craving doesn't signal your need for a sugar or starch fix, but it's coming from a place of habit or acclimatization. When your expectation isn't met, your craving intensifies.

You Numb Out and Eat Quickly

When you're an emotional eater, you treat food as a mere distraction. It becomes your temporary escape from the world. We are all susceptible to anxiety and overthinking, and these are things we experience often. Unfortunately, when you train your mind to associate food with diversions, you start eating as soon as an undesirable thought enters your mind.

Eventually, you tune out entirely when you eat and can't focus on your meal. You don't take the time to notice how the food tastes, chew it properly, enjoy it, or notice your fullness. We resort to unhealthy coping mechanisms like stress eating because we find it difficult to cope with stressful situations and thoughts. Even though your body turns to the easiest, quickest, and most comforting diversion it knows, it fails to pay attention to it. Our subconscious minds want to turn away from anything associated with the stress we're experiencing, even if it's our source of distraction and comfort.

You Eat Right after You Experience an Emotional Event

No matter the emotions an event induces, whether negative or positive, you eat afterward. Food is your reward, pain reliever, and distraction. Your brain links it to feelings of happiness, anxiety, and sadness, so it only makes sense that you'd feel the urge to eat whenever you're celebrating or grieving. Happy events might feel incomplete if they're not complemented by food. Similarly, you tell yourself you won't feel better unless you eat chocolate, ice cream, or your comfort food. Food is like an anchor; you're always drawn to it because it keeps you grounded. It alleviates the intense emotions you're experiencing.

You Feel Guilty after You Eat

Your brain can tell when you are stress eating, even if you aren't consciously aware. Your mind signals your body is hungry and needs to eat. It also signals to your body you're stressed, and this is when you feel the compulsion to relieve your anxiety and fight-or-flight response by eating. Hence, you feel guilty and ashamed after eating.

You Feel a Sudden Hunger Pang

While it doesn't always accompany physical hunger, emotional eating sometimes manifests as sudden hunger pangs. It can feel overwhelming, overpowering, and accompanied by a sense of urgency. The difference between emotional eating and regular hunger is the latter build up more gradually. While it takes more time to satisfy regular hunger, emotional hunger offers instant gratification, followed by guilt.

Stress-eating is very challenging to overcome, especially if you don't have a support system to encourage you throughout the process. There are numerous misconceptions about disordered eating habits, which leave you feeling disheartened and misunderstood. If you talk about your stress-eating habits, you might get a response as shallow as, "'oh, me too. I had a whole bag of chips while I was working on this report yesterday. Can you imagine?" Chewing your feelings away makes you feel guilty and ashamed. It could even cause you to self-isolate because social gatherings make you anxious. You constantly worry about what and when you're going to eat, making it impossible to enjoy the time you spend with your loved ones or focus on any task. We're here to tell you that you aren't alone, and there are so many things you can do to turn your situation around.

Key Takeaways

- The release of cortisol, a stress-related hormone, in the body can stimulate your appetite and encourage stress-eating.
- The inability to manage your emotions can cause you to adopt emotional eating as a coping mechanism.
- You can regulate your food cravings by ensuring you incorporate adequate healthy fats, sugars, and carbs into your diet.
- We stress eat when we subconsciously think of food as a reward.

- An unhealthy preoccupation with food is a very common sign of stress eating.
- Restricting your food intake can cause you to eat past fullness and promote an unhealthy relationship with food.

Now that you've determined if you're a stress eater, read the following chapters for tips on managing your emotions, eating habits, and techniques to stop compulsive eating.

4

HOW TO STOP COMPULSIVE EATING

"*Binge-ing is such an emotionally frenetic activity that no other concerns can exist in the same space. It is a hell that people who are food-sensitive are familiar with, and because it is known, it is therefore not so terrifying as some of the problems that are outside our control. Problems like divorce, illness, death.*" — Geneen Roth, Feeding the Hungry Heart: The Experience of Compulsive Eating

As someone who's got a love-hate relationship with food, you've likely tried many times to get rid of your binge eating habits. However, considering you're reading this book, it's safe to assume the techniques you tried haven't worked out well for you, which is perfectly normal. Generic tips and tricks cannot always help you gain control over your unhealthy eating habits. Compulsive eating is a serious matter and should be taken as such. Nonetheless, there's no reason to lose hope or give up on yourself because a few techniques from the internet couldn't help you.

Dealing with compulsive eating is a long journey that requires consistency, determination, and resolve. To change this stubborn habit, you must make extensive lifestyle changes - only then will you be successful. This chapter provides a complete guide to establishing a foundation to eliminate the unhealthy habit of compulsive eating, starting with learning what compulsive eating is and how it relates to stress eating. Once you're aware of the psychology behind this behavior, you'll be much more suited to dealing with it. To further help you out, the chapter includes some tried and tested techniques to help you minimize or eliminate your compulsive eating habits.

Compulsive Eating: The Basics

Compulsive overeating is a stage of stress eating when a person eats to feel happy but feels a loss of control. As a result, they start eating again, and the cycle continues. Compulsive eating is worse than stress eating because it becomes a full-blown eating disorder. While stress eating is done to cope with stress or other negative feelings, compulsive eating becomes uncontrollable. People dealing with this disorder binge eat or engage in grazing behavior.

Compulsive eating usually develops slowly and could be initiated at an early age. For instance, a kid might turn to food when sad and slowly but surely, become dependent on food for their happiness. In many instances, adults suffer from this problem due to body-image issues or bullying. Like stress eating, compulsive eating is developed due to an unhealthy coping mechanism of drowning feelings by eating excessively.

Long-Term Health Risks

Many severe health risks are associated with binge eating and compulsive eating disorders. These health issues cause short-term and long-term problems, so seeking treatment and doing everything possible to break this habit is critical. Some health risks include:

- Obesity/ unhealthy weight gain
- High blood pressure
- Diabetes
- Gastrointestinal issues
- High cholesterol
- Arthritis
- Sleep problems
- Pregnancy issues
- Depression
- Social isolation
- Crippling anxiety

Overcoming Compulsive Eating

Given the stigma associated with overeating, creating a healthy relationship with food can be challenging. When you become overly conscious of your eating habits, you're bound to feel guilty, even if you're not doing anything wrong, which frequently triggers compulsive eating habits. Nevertheless, you can adopt a few tricks and techniques to improve your relationship with food. However, if you have a severe eating disorder, you might need professional medical assistance to successfully break your compulsive eating patterns. Listed below are the most basic techniques to incorporate into your life to subdue your unhealthy eating habits.

1. **Identify Triggers**

Like binge-eating behavior varies from person to person, the triggers of this behavior also differ for everyone. Therefore, the first step towards overcoming compulsive eating behaviors is identifying the triggers that lead to this conduct. For most people, these triggers are negative emotions, including but not limited to stress. People are often attracted to tasty food items when feeling low and want to drown their feelings. This behavior is often referred to as "eating your emotions" because people eat to suppress their emotions. However, this unhealthy coping mechanism leads to guilt and even depression.

Another trigger for this behavior is the restrictions we impose on ourselves, for instance, a diet. Most people who go on strict diets gain more weight than they lose. It is the result of restricting certain food items, making resisting them more challenging. Unrealistic diets hurt you more than they help; developing a healthy yet reasonable diet plan is crucial. Have you ever tried a quick weight loss diet and failed? The reason is that by restricting certain food items, these diets trigger your binge eating habits more intensely. Research proves that people who restrict themselves from eating tend to eat more than the average person. So, controlling your diet makes you a binge eater. However, it does not mean you should give up on your unhealthy eating habits. Instead, try other, more effective techniques for improving your eating lifestyle.

One more common trigger of binge eating is becoming self-conscious of your body. When you feel bloated or fat, you'll let your negative self-image take over reality, and you lose hope, leading to a sense of failure and a lack of self-care, which equals compulsive eating. You don't know that when you weigh yourself every other day, you're bound to have weight fluctuations. It is scientifically impossible to gain or lose a few pounds in a day. That would require consuming more than 3,500 calories, which is far more than the average diet. So, where do these fluctuations come from? The weight changes are water retention or hormonal changes, not the weight you're gaining. Keeping this in mind, you will become less weight conscious and actively work towards a healthy lifestyle without the added stress of weight gain. Weighing yourself once a month is enough to stay aware of any weight changes and will keep your mind at peace.

Once you've identified the triggers that send you on binge eating sprees, you should completely avoid them or gradually incorporate them back into your life. This should be systematically done for trigger foods so you don't risk having another binge eating episode. This will be discussed in detail in a later chapter. For other triggers, the best you can do is avoid certain stressful situations until you can be confident that they won't trigger your disorder.

1. **Change Your Diet**

What does the word "diet" bring to your mind? Weight loss? Better health? Restricting junk food? Counting calories? Are you tired of restricting yourself from eating, trying to lose weight, and going on extreme and slightly unhealthy diets? All this needs to stop now. You were probably not expecting this advice from a book on healthy eating advice, right? As discussed in the previous section, dieting does you more harm than good. While the short-term results of a diet might seem wonderful, in the long term, you'll almost always gain the weight back, along with a couple of unhealthy habits.

Restricting your diet to lose weight leads to your metabolic system being in a hyper-controlled state. Your body loses all sensations associated with hunger and feelings of fullness. So, if you're someone with compulsive eating habits, it is essential that you do not restrict certain food items or go on extremely suppressive diets. For instance, if you love chocolate, but your diet tells you not to indulge in it, you'll most likely opt for a low-calorie yogurt, but later, you'll crave chocolate again and consume more chocolate than you normally would. This behavior can only be controlled by allowing yourself to enjoy a few pieces of chocolate fully so your brain doesn't believe it's a restricted item.

By doing this, you replace the fear of not having a certain food with the satisfaction of knowing you can truly enjoy what you like to eat. Of course, this technique is difficult to adopt if some food items are especially triggering for your compulsive eating habits. Nevertheless, they can still be incorporated into your diet gradually. Certain guidelines you should follow to adapt your diet to manage compulsive eating better include:

- Acknowledge that you're allowed to eat anything; nothing is restricted. However, some food items are part of your daily diet, while others can be consumed occasionally.

- Stay aware of your hunger, and stop eating as soon as you feel full.
- Avoid eating for comfort or with negative emotions, and adopt other healthy coping methods instead (discussed in another chapter).
- Don't weigh yourself more than once a month.
- When you eat something, enjoy the taste of your food instead of gobbling it down.

You don't have to follow a perfect diet to be in control of your eating habits. Categorizing food as good or bad, healthy or unhealthy, can affect your relationship with it. Instead, settle with assigning certain food items for occasional consumption while others can be on the menu regularly. Eating well can be a tricky thing sometimes. There are so many diet plans and nutritional therapies that it becomes confusing. The best option is to stick to a balanced plate. Half the plate should be filled with veggies, a quarter with grains, and the remaining portion with protein.

Having variety is also key to healthy eating habits. If you have a variety of foods, some reassuring to you, you'll more likely stick to your regular diet. If not, you'll be drawn towards binge eating. Reintroducing trigger foods is also tricky, but it can be done when surrounded by friends or family. For instance, if a chocolate dessert is a trigger food for you, eat it at a party or an event surrounded by people. When you observe others eating the same food and enjoying it, it'll be a much less stressful experience and won't draw you towards binge-ing.

Once you stop counting calories and trying to restrict your diet, you can start eating food items to help you fill up quickly. Typically, high-protein and high-fiber foods are very fulfilling. Incorporating these food items into your diet will ensure there's no space for unhealthy or binge-eating habits. Here are a few tips for feeling full quicker:

1. Increase your fiber consumption by replacing the food items you already have on your daily menu with more nutritious food. For instance, whole wheat pasta has more fiber than refined flour pasta. Take time to read the nutrition information provided for each product, and pick the ones with the most nutrition.

2. In addition to fiber, protein helps satisfy hunger. Therefore, add a high-protein food item to every meal of the day. These can include cheese, eggs, fish, poultry, or legumes. Most people overlook protein source food items in the morning and noon, which leads to daytime cravings.

3. Sugary drinks are far less sustaining than sugary food items and only add to your calories. Don't limit or restrict these drinks, but keep an eye on how much you consume. A good idea is to replace these beverages with tea, milk, water, coffee, and plant-based drinks.

4. Add lots of vegetables to your diet. The more veggies you consume, the less hungry you'll be. A vegetable salad works best as a daytime snack.

5. Incorporating healthy snacks into your diet is the best way to curb unhealthy cravings during the day. Ensure the snacks are delicious and not only nutritious to keep away from unhealthy snacks. Some ideas for these snacks:

- Grapes and cottage cheese

- Dried cranberries and almonds
- A peanut butter sandwich with whole-grain bread
- Crackers and hummus
- Vegetable juice and a hardboiled egg
- Flavored Greek yogurt

1. **Incorporate Physical Exercise**

It's a well-known fact that physical exercise is good for your physical and mental health. Many people incorporate exercise into their lifestyles to improve their health and to be happier. Regularly exercising generates endorphins, neurotransmitters that positively impact your mood, sleep quality, and stress and help with anxiety management. In particular, outdoor exercise and yoga have been linked to enhanced mood and quality of life.

For people dealing with compulsive eating, physical exercise has proven beneficial, considering it helps them lose weight, with fitness, feel in control of their life, and not turn towards food as a coping mechanism. Aerobic exercises can significantly help lessen anxiety, depression, stress, and panic symptoms, making a person feel relaxed and in control.

Incorporating physical exercise into your routine doesn't mean you must adopt an exhausting fitness program. On the contrary, you shouldn't integrate exercise into your life just to lose weight. Instead, you should focus on the happiness and peace it brings. Start with a 15-minute walk every day, and develop your exercise routine from there. There's no need to rush this process; only do it to make yourself feel better.

Some tips for more exercise:

- Find a physical activity you like. If you don't like gyms or working out, that's fine. Look for something that brings you a feeling of control. Join a dance program, a tennis club, swim lessons, or jog daily. Anything to get you moving will work.
- Exercise with your family or friends to keep yourself motivated and engaged. It's super boring to exercise alone some people, and they usually give up. Take a friend or loved one with you when you walk, jog, or swim to ensure this doesn't happen. You can also find fun physical activities like skating, playing ball, etc.
- If you're serious about including exercise in your daily routine, it's a good idea to hire a personal trainer to keep you motivated. They will ensure you follow a suitable plan from the beginning that considers your limits and pain points.
- Make a list of realistic goals you think you can achieve. It's useless to set unreasonable expectations. Start by walking 15-minutes a day, and keep adding bigger goals as you improve.
- Record your physical progress, and it'll keep you motivated. Note down little things like not being breathless after a walk or a run. Results like this will make you want to continue this lifestyle.
- Here's an exercise routine you can try as a beginner:
- Day 1: Cardio for 25 minutes, strength exercises for 10 to 20 minutes, and stretch for 5 minutes.
- Day 2: 15-minute walk, stretching exercise for 10 to 20 minutes.

- Day 3: Cardio (Jogging) for 20 minutes, strength exercise for 10 to 15 minutes, and stretch for 5 minutes.
- Day 4: Rest
- Day 5: 15-minute brisk walk, stretching exercise for 5 to 10 minutes.

1. **Practice Mindfulness**

Mindfulness, managing emotions, practicing mindful eating, and stress tolerance techniques help reduce binge-eating habits. Once you learn how to deal with your stress, the uncontrollable cravings will not bother you anymore. Managing stress and mindful eating will be discussed in later chapters, but for now, let's discuss how you can use mindfulness to stop compulsive eating and let go of this habit for good.

Mindfulness means getting in touch with your emotions and behaviors and accepting them without judgment. It is a state that transcends your normal mental state and can only be achieved by taking full control of your mind and body. While many people are hesitant to try mindfulness techniques to treat their eating disorders, these techniques have worked wonders for others.

These techniques can help deal with any binge-eating urges you get, whether during the recovery process or after. A mental state has to be reached that helps you focus on the present moment to achieve mindfulness. Calmly focus on all your emotions, feelings, and bodily sensations at the moment, and accept and embrace them.

Accepting your negative emotions will ultimately help you overcome your eating problems. You'll no longer need to find other coping methods because you'll finally be strong enough to deal with your emotions, no matter how intense. Sounds impossible, right? Well, it's not that hard to achieve. This method is so effective against compulsive eating because the main cause of binge eating is guilt and loss of control. Once you learn to accept your feelings, you'll no longer feel guilty for eating something.

You won't be compelled to eat more to cope with your guilt. The cycle will finally be broken. In addition, when you're mindful of your bodily sensations, you won't have to rely on emotional cues to eat or not eat. You'll know when your body needs food and when you're being drawn towards food for other reasons. With further mindfulness and slow-eating exercises, you can break your habit of reaction eating triggered by intense emotions.

Tips for developing your personalized mindful practice:

- It's best to start small instead of setting overly ambitious goals. While starting with 1-hour meditation sessions each day might seem productive, you'll most likely encounter laziness and distractions if you try to commit so much time to this task. A 5-minute meditation practice is ideal for a beginner.
- Since you're getting started with your meditation practice, finding a comfortable place to practice mindfulness is best. For instance, wake up early in the morning, and find a quiet place away from everyone else for your meditation practice. Ensure

you meditate at the same time every day to stay consistent.

- Set a timer for however long you decide to meditate. It will keep you from worrying about the duration of the meditation practice during the actual practice. All your focus should be on meditation.
- Diaphragmatic breathing is perfect for mindful meditation. However, before you implement it completely into your practice, you must practice it. Don't hold your breath during the practice. Instead, try simpler breathing exercises.
- Accept that your mind is bound to wander during the practice. The purpose of meditation is not to completely shut the world out but to increase awareness about your body and feelings. It's okay if your thoughts start to divert. Simply bring your focus back to the matter at hand.
- As a beginner, you'll often worry about what you should and shouldn't be doing during the practice. If you struggle with this, listening to a guided meditation is better.

Key Takeaways

- Understanding triggers for your overeating habits is the first step toward improving your habits and yourself.
- These triggers vary from person to person but are most often associated with restricted food, body image, and stressful situations.

- Going on a diet is not the way to stop overeating, but gradually changing your diet is. Diets make you feel restricted, but incorporating healthier eating patterns will empower you.
- Keep a balanced plate for your diet, including plenty of proteins, fibers, and carbohydrates.
- Adding physical exercise seems like basic advice when trying to lose weight, but it helps you gain a healthier lifestyle and will get you to manage your overeating habits.
- Finally, be mindful of what you eat. Mindfulness will help you solve many issues associated with your eating struggles. It will be discussed in more detail in an upcoming chapter.

Compulsive eating can quickly turn into a full-fledged eating disorder if not dealt with at an early stage. The severe health issues that arise from this disorder should never be underestimated; therefore, proper steps should be taken to stop compulsive eating habits. Hopefully, the techniques detailed in this chapter helped you get a gist of how you can regain control over your body, mind, and eating habits.

The next chapter includes some more tricks to help with a compulsive eating disorder and simple techniques to incorporate into your life for coping with stress eating and similar disorders.

5

10 PRACTICAL TECHNIQUES TO STOP COMPULSIVE EATING IN 30 DAYS

"*No food will ever hurt you as much as an unhealthy mind.*" — Brittany Burgunder

This chapter explores 10 techniques to help you stop compulsive eating in 30 days. You'll learn each method and understand its benefits. You'll also learn step-by-step instructions on implementing each technique.

1 Keep a Food Diary

A food diary allows you to log what you drink and eat every day. It helps you better understand your eating habits and brings more awareness to what you eat. If you seek professional help, showing your doctor your food diary enables them to tailor their advice and treatment plan to your needs.

You can use many online apps to log your food and drink consumption. However, putting it down in writing allows you to format your log to suit your needs. Choose a small notebook to carry around with you throughout the day.

There are 7 main pieces of information you should write down each time you eat or drink. Create a table for each day with 7 columns and as many rows as you need. The top row in the table should be filled in as follows: how much, what kind, where, with who, activity, and mood. The amount could be measured in weight (4 ounces of tuna), volume (½ a cup of milk), or the number of pieces or items (2 eggs or 15 chips).

Be as specific as possible when you mention the food or beverage. Remember to add condiments, sauces, and toppings. If you eat salad, for instance, mention the ingredients and the dressing. If you eat fries, don't forget to include the ketchup and mayonnaise. Other extras could include sugar, butter, honey, etc.

Ensure to mention the exact location where you eat and drink. If you're at work, are you eating at the cafeteria or in your office? If you're at home, which room are you eating in? If you're eating out, mention the name of the restaurant. Write down the names of the people you were with, even if they aren't eating. Don't just write "friends," "family," or "co-workers," write down their names. If you're alone, mention that.

In the following column, write down what you're doing while eating or drinking. If you're working, which task are you working on? What movie or TV show are you watching? Which songs are you listening to? Mention how you feel while eating or drinking. Are you bored, angry, annoyed, sad, or happy?

Our mood and everything around us influences our food choices. For instance, you might feel compelled to eat "clean" around your co-workers. However, you overeat when you're out with friends due to peer pressure. You notice you make better food choices at home because you have less time to meal prep for work. Some people eat more than usual when watching TV.

You must log everything you eat or drink regardless of how insignificant it seems. You should also write everything down immediately because you'll likely forget if you leave it for later. Be specific when mentioning what you eat. For example, if you have an omelet, write that down instead of "eggs." Always mention an estimate of the quantity of food you're consuming.

Keeping a food diary can be very mentally and emotionally taxing. There will be days when you are happy about your efforts. However, some days won't look as good, making you feel guilty. Remember, you're not keeping a food diary to beat yourself up but to find a solution. Recovery is never linear. You might feel compelled to lie on your log, but it won't benefit you. Your diary must be true if you desire to put compulsive eating behind you.

Here is an example of how you'd log breakfast into your food diary:

How Much: 1 medium egg
What Kind: Omelet
When: 9:45 am
Where: Dining table
With Whom: alone
Activity: Watching 'Friends'
Mood: Happy

How Much: 1 slice

What Kind: Toasted brown bread
When: 9:45 am
Where: Dining table
With Whom: alone
Activity: Watching 'Friends'
Mood: Happy

How Much: 1 cup
What Kind: coffee
When: 9:45 am
Where: Dining table
With Whom: alone
Activity: Watching 'Friends'
Mood: Happy

2 De-Stress Daily

It goes without saying that the first thing you need to do to combat stress-eating habits is to manage your stress. Getting your fair share of daily exercise will not end stress but will help you cope. Exercise can help you clarify your thoughts and alleviate the intensity of your emotions. Go for a run, hit the gym, dance it out, or take up kickboxing classes. It doesn't matter what you do as long as you're active for at least 20 minutes every day.

You should also connect with nature every day. Open your windows to let the fresh air and natural light flow into your home each morning. Go for a walk outside and observe the different shades of green on the leaves. You can go cloud- or bird-watching. Go stargazing in the evenings. Being in nature helps you stay grounded and enhances your mood.

Time is our most valuable possession. We're the most stressed whenever we feel like we don't have control over certain aspects of our lives. While it's not possible to control everything, you can choose where and how to spend your time. Learning time management techniques and using scheduling tools can help you take the reins over your life.

Take time for yourself every day. Use this time to do something you enjoy; meditate, reflect, or practice self-care. You could also sit in a quiet room by yourself if that's what you need. Use this time to unwind and re-energize.

3 Treat Yourself with Kindness and Compassion

It could be very easy to fall into the self-blame loop when dealing with compulsive eating. You scold yourself for eating past the number of servings you've permitted yourself or feel remorseful after reflecting on your food choices. You tell yourself you have to do better tomorrow, and the cycle continues.

Before you set out on the road to recovery, you need to understand two things: 1. Recovery isn't a linear journey. Some days will be good, and others will be bad. You will inevitably relapse before you fully heal. 2. There's nothing wrong with you. You don't need to be "fixed." None of the many people who struggle with compulsive eating choose to do this to themselves. While you don't actively choose to become a compulsive eater, you do have the power to turn your life around. You developed stress-eating habits because you didn't know how to cope better. Perhaps you were brought up in an environment plagued by diet culture.

Start by forgiving yourself and learning to treat yourself with kindness. Take care of your body and recognize when you need a break. Book a massage session, take a bubble bath, go for a walk, stretch, do yoga, or even take a nap. Improving your physical state can boost your self-compassion.

Write a letter to yourself describing how compulsive eating makes you feel and how it affects your life. Avoid blaming yourself (or anyone else) for this habit. Externalizing your thoughts and emotions can relieve some of the weight you've been carrying.

Address yourself as you would talk to your friend. What if your best friend told you they struggle with compulsive eating and hate themselves for it? You likely wouldn't agree with them and tell them their eating habits don't define them. You'll encourage them, approach them with compassion, and tell them you'll be by their side throughout this journey.

If you'd do that for a friend, why won't you do it for yourself? You're the only person who's been by your side for every moment of every day. While you might have had a support system by your side, you're the one who's managed to pull yourself out of every difficult situation.

4 Lose the Food Rules

This might seem counter-intuitive, but as mentioned in previous chapters, you must trust that your body knows what it's doing. Restricting your food intake is not the right way to deal with compulsive eating because it only reinforces unhealthy eating habits. You need to build a healthy relationship with food to stop stress-eating, which requires permitting yourself to eat.

Creating food rules and labeling meals as "good" and "bad" causes you to develop a fear of food and feel deprived. You're worried that allowing yourself to eat cookies for dessert encourages you to empty the entire box. However, if you eat cookies whenever you want to, you can stop when you're satiated. If you crave cookies and eat cucumbers instead, you won't stop thinking about the unopened pack in the pantry. You'll finally cave, and instead of eating a few cookies, like you would've if you hadn't been restricted, your brain fears you won't eat cookies the next time you crave them, so you cannot stop eating.

You should eat whenever you're hungry instead of forcing yourself to stick to certain meal times. Your body and hunger cues don't operate on a schedule; you're not a machine. Instead of trying to control your hunger, listen to it. We are all born with the ability to recognize our hunger. Children can naturally tell if they're hungry and when they're full. Unfortunately, we seem to lose this sense as we grow up due to external factors.

Our parents had good intentions when they told us to eat every last bite before we left the dining table. However, being forced to eat past our fullness taught us that external factors, such as eating the entire plate or until we gain the approval of others, are more important than internal stimuli (signals of fullness), which we learned to ignore.

As we grew older, diet culture taught us about calories. We learned that reaching a certain number meant we were done eating instead of eating until we were satisfied.

It's time to lose these rules and start listening to your hunger, fullness, and satisfaction cues. It will be hard, especially if you've lived by these rules for most of your life. While it's great to go all in, you don't need to if you don't feel ready. Being sustainable with your efforts is all that matters, even if you're taking baby steps.

5 Try Mindful Eating

Practicing mindful eating is a great way to fix your relationship with food. This technique refers to being present in the moment as you eat. Mindful eaters don't just consume food; they experience it.

Practicing mindful eating requires eliminating any distractions, such as books, TV, phone, or even conversations while eating. Use this as an opportunity to observe and reflect on what you're eating. Notice the texture of the food, its aroma, the different flavors, and how your hunger cues change throughout the meal. Enjoy the whole eating experience.

Mindful eating encourages you to take the time to savor your meals, allowing you to determine which foods you dislike and those you really enjoy. This technique also enables you to become more attuned to your body's hunger and fullness signals.

Most importantly, being a mindful eater allows you to bring awareness to your food choices. Are you choosing to eat this food because you're bored? Are you eating it because you genuinely like it? Is it because you're starving to the point where you'll eat anything? Do you think eating it will make you feel emotionally better?

Here are some questions to answer while eating.

- Am I really enjoying this meal? Does it satisfy my current cravings?
- How is my appetite changing now that I'm eating? Am I less hungry? Do I feel fuller?
- Was I really hungry when I decided to eat? If not, why did I choose to eat (stress-eating, boredom, craving, peer pressure, meal-time rule, etc?)
- What flavors, aromas, and textures am I picking up?
- Is this what I wanted to eat, or am I eating it because it's available?
- Which problem did I think eating this food would fix? Did it fix it like I thought it would?
- Which emotions are this food bringing up for me? Am I feeling happy, annoyed, or guilty now that I'm eating this?

It's normal to feel difficulty answering these questions. Approach them with a sense of curiosity rather than from a place of judgment. If it helps, write down your answers in a journal, it trains you to determine why you make certain food choices and whether your coping mechanism is in action.

6 Get Rid of the Labels

You give food unnecessary amounts of power by labelling your food as "good" or "bad." While some food options are healthier than others due to their high nutritional value, they won't boost your health if you eat them once. Similarly, you won't develop a health condition if you choose to have pizza for lunch today.

When we label a certain food item as "good," we permit ourselves to consume as much of it as we want when essentially, too much of anything can be detrimental. Labeling foods as "bad" can make us fearful of them, leading to the restriction (and the cycle begins). Besides, it's human nature to want something if you know you can't have it.

Getting rid of the labels and embracing all foods in your diet allows you to control your intake more effectively. Knowing you can eat anything whenever you want lowers the chances of binge eating and eliminates guilt.

You become habituated when you expose yourself to all foods and incorporate them into your regular diet. It means these food options become less appealing, which helps you limit your compulsive-eating episodes.

However, embracing various food is not enough if you guilt-trip yourself afterward. You might feel triggered after enjoying an unhealthy meal or eating too much dessert. Your efforts to create a healthy relationship with food will be futile if you resume punishing yourself for eating certain foods. You don't need to eat "clean" or cut out calories the following day to compensate for what you eat, and neither do you need to remind yourself repeatedly that you're "out of control."

7 Avoid Justifying Your Food Choices

No one needs to know why you eat what you eat or when you eat it, whether you have oats and fruits for breakfast or a chocolate cake at 3 am. You don't even need to justify your food choices to yourself. It's okay to reach out for the ice cream tub without telling yourself, "it's fine if I eat ice cream because I had salad for lunch today." Eat what you want to eat whenever you want to eat it, and move on. "Because I felt like it" is a good enough reason.

8 Reframe Your Thoughts

Having negative thoughts about food is what reinforces our negative relationship with it. So, learning to reframe your thoughts can help you fix your disordered eating patterns.

5 Methods to Reframe Your Negative Thought

Stewing

You decide to lose the food rules and have a few cookies because you were craving them. As you are about to reach into your pantry, your brain hits you with the thought, "do you know how many calories a few cookies have? Cookies are bad." You remind yourself there are no good or bad foods, but you can't help dwelling over how horrible cookies are for you. This indecision causes you to lose sight of the bigger picture - fixing your relationship with food.

To reframe similar thoughts, you must recognize intrusive thoughts as soon as they enter your brain. Intentionally stop them dead in their tracks and replace these thoughts with better ones. Remember why you're doing this, and tell yourself that having a few cookies won't affect your health.

All or Nothing

All-or-nothing thoughts force you to see the world in black or white. You think your efforts are either extremely successful or dreadful failures. Let's say someone follows a very strict diet but has a scoop of ice cream. They decide it has ruined their diet, so they might as well eat the entire tub.

All-or-nothing thinking is extremely destructive. Making unhealthy food choices doesn't mean you've failed. It merely means you're a human who's striving for balance and eating whatever feels right at a given moment.

Magnifying

WE OFTEN DRAW VERY unreasonable conclusions based on limited past experiences. We overgeneralize and make the situation seem bigger than it is. For instance, you tell yourself you will never be able to stop eating if you allow yourself to eat whatever you want.

To reframe this thought, you must remind yourself that you can change the situation. Forgive yourself for the last time you binge-ate. You probably overate the last time because you constantly told yourself you couldn't eat the food item. However, the situation will be different now that you permit yourself to eat anything you want.

Personalization

This refers to thinking that everything happening around you is about you. Personalization is taking everything, including people's words and behaviors, personally. It is very unhealthy because it leads to self-blame and doubt. For example, someone struggling with disordered eating could consider an innocent question like "Do you have burgers for lunch again?" as a negative comment on their eating habits or body. However, the person asking might be harmlessly asking if they're not craving anything else.

You must realize not everything that happens or is said around you has something to do with you. Before you jump to conclusions, remember you don't know what others are truly thinking.

Fortune-Telling

THIS IS when you assume the results of a situation before it happens. It also applies to thinking you know what someone else is thinking about. Anticipating that you will gain a few pounds because you made "bad" food choices today is very unreasonable.

Start thinking positively. Remember that everything you do today will lead to a better, pain-free future.

9 Connect with People

Many people find it the hardest to deal with compulsive eating when they're free and home alone. Therefore, you need to ensure you're surrounded by a good network of friends and family. This way, you can reach out to them whenever you feel your stress-eating triggers rising. Ask them to do stress-relieving, calming, or distracting activities together. Talk to them when you need to put your mind at ease or when you need them to help you put your thoughts into perspective.

10 Learn from Setbacks

If you have a compulsive eating episode, forgive yourself and move on. You can always start the next day again and learn from what happened. Any healing journey accompanies setbacks and relapses. However, the most important thing to do is to avoid feeling discouraged when this happens. Reflect on your triggers and think about how you can prevent this from happening again. Remind yourself of all the positive changes you've already made, and you're getting closer to your goal every day.

Key Takeaways

- You must practice these habits together for 30 days to see the desired results.
- Keep a food diary, make sure you're de-stressed, and self-compassion will help you identify and eliminate your stress-eating triggers.
- Losing the food rules, practicing mindful eating, avoiding labeling food as "good" or "bad," and realizing you don't need to justify your food choices will fix your relationship with food.
- Finally, reframing your thoughts, building a supportive network of friends and family, and learning from your setbacks helps you maintain your efforts.

Now that you know how to stop compulsive eating, read the following chapter to learn to manage your emotions. It is one of the most important of cutting off unhealthy coping mechanisms.

6

MANAGING YOUR EMOTIONS

"I don't want to be at the mercy of my emotions. I want to use them, to enjoy them, and to dominate them." Oscar Wilde

Are you in control of your emotions, or are your emotions in control of you?

You have probably heard the saying, "don't be a slave to your emotions." Emotions can sometimes be overwhelming, whether anger, grief, or even happiness. It feels like someone is behind the wheel, making you say or do things you wouldn't normally say or do. Your reactions can take you by surprise, and when emotions are left unchecked and unmanaged, you lose control, leading to compulsive eating.

This chapter discusses how emotions can cause stress eating, how to recognize these emotions, and how to manage them.

Emotions and Compulsive Eating

Comfort has a different meaning for each person. Whether it is an object or a place, everyone has something or somewhere that makes them feel calm and at peace. While it is normal to have a favorite food that brings you comfort, like a dish that reminds you of home or your grandmother's secret recipe, it isn't healthy as a coping mechanism during moments of stress or anxiety. It is similar to smoking, a compulsive behavior you resort to without applying logical thinking.

Food and emotions have always had complicated relationships and usually influence each other. Positive and negative emotions can impact your eating habits. Positive emotions, like pleasure, influence people to overeat as they believe food maintains this feeling. On the other hand, negative emotions affect your sense of self-control, resulting in compulsive eating. Food provides an escape from the environment, resorting to overeating instead of confronting the source of unhappiness.

When you are in pain, you want a distraction or something to take away the pain. It is similar to the relationship between addicts and drugs. As mentioned, emotional hunger resembles a void inside you, and food is the only way to fill it. Various things can create this void, like a breakup, the death of a loved one, or losing your job. You replace this pain with a different feeling, fullness, by overeating.

We all have objects associated with memories, like a gift from our first love, an item that belonged to a deceased parent, or our childhood pictures. Turning to these objects can bring warmth and nostalgia. Food has a similar effect. For instance, chocolate ice cream might remind you of when your dad picked you and your siblings up from school and treated you to ice cream. Or caramel popcorn could remind you of sleepovers when you and your friends spent the whole night eating popcorn and watching movies. You can't go back in time to relive these moments, but food can bring back the associated emotions. When you have a bad day and want to improve your mood, you will be drawn to foods that bring back comfort and warm memories. You eat and eat until you fill the emptiness. As these overwhelming emotions take charge, you cannot control your food intake. Loss of control is key here. When people struggle to manage or control their emotions, they can't control their impulses, which, in this case, is compulsive eating.

People with stress, anxiety, or depression often resort to compulsive eating to cope with their symptoms. They believe food can help them deal with daily stressful situations by providing them with a temporary sense of comfort and pleasure. Food becomes a coping mechanism because you believe it is the only thing that can bring you the positive emotions you desperately need.

In other words, food is delicious and negative emotions are unpleasant. Not everyone manages their emotions, so they avoid them instead. They turn to the one simple thing they believe can bring them pleasure, which is food. Even though this relief is momentary, they become addicted to these small moments of peace that food brings them.

Identifying the Negative Emotions

As mentioned, each person has triggers that drive them to overeat. Negative emotions are strong triggers driving a person to consume food mindlessly. Compulsive eating becomes a natural reaction to negative external stimuli or emotions. You might be unaware that your hunger is more emotional than physical. So, you must first recognize what triggers your unhealthy eating habits to manage your feelings.

Stress

We can't talk about stress eating without mentioning stress. As mentioned, stress is one of the main triggers of compulsive eating. Stress can be subjective, meaning you will find a situation stressful while others don't. Some people are more laid back and don't get stressed easily, while any minor inconvenience can stress others out. It means you are more in control of your stress than it is of you. You have the power to prevent a situation or person from getting to you and ruining your day. There is no denying that life is stressful, whether school, work, or family, and it is easy to lose yourself in this negative emotion. However, it is your view and reaction to a situation that determines if it's worth stressing about or not. Even the most stressful situations can be dealt with by healthy and effective coping mechanisms rather than temporary ones, like food.

Instead of giving in to this emotion, make some changes in your life to help you avoid certain stressful situations or lessen their impact. For instance, if your job puts you under pressure, look for a new one. If this is impossible at the moment, find healthy coping mechanisms to equip you better to handle the stress of your job. For instance, yoga and meditation are effective methods of making you feel calm and centered.

Sadness

We all experience sadness at different levels. Your sadness over losing a parent isn't the same as your sadness over losing your job. Sadness is associated with loss, and many people resort to food to fill the void a loss leaves them. It is true that time heals everything, but in the meantime, food can numb the pain and distract you from your sadness. Since overeating is often accompanied by guilt and shame, you will feel worse. Various effective ways to help you cope with sadness are long-lasting - Exercising, volunteer work, meditation, journaling, or reaching out to a friend; if your sadness results from depression, seeking professional help is essential.

Happiness

Like negative emotions, positive ones like happiness can also cause overeating. Compulsive eaters are driven by their emotions. Any time you feel a strong emotion, you reach out for food. It has become a friend you turn to when you need a shoulder to cry on or share your happy moments with. In every culture, food has always been a part of celebrations-on birthdays, we eat cake; on Thanksgiving, we eat turkey; and on Halloween, we eat candy. It is a learned behavior we grow up with, so happiness is celebrated by eating. Celebrating certain events with food or treating yourself to a good meal now and then is normal. However, if you only treat or reward yourself with food, you need to change this behavior. For instance, you get promoted and want to do something nice for your family.

Instead of taking them to dinner, buy them a small gift. Or, if you achieved a goal and want to treat yourself, book a day at a spa.

Boredom

One of the main tips dietitians often give is to ask yourself if you are eating because you are hungry or bored. Boredom has always been associated with food. Even non-compulsive eaters grab a snack or order a pizza when they have nothing better to do. If this happens on rare occasions, it is fine. However, if your only solution to boredom is eating, it is a problem. You can do many things to battle boredom, like working out, reading, or watching a movie. Compulsive eaters turn to food because it is their coping mechanism. It is the comfort zone they seek whenever they experience any negative emotions.

Moreover, healthy activities are more satisfying and significantly impact your life. For instance, if you schedule a time to read or join a gym, these activities will prevent boredom and keep you mentally and physically healthy. Don't give in to boredom by running to the fridge. Find something you enjoy and do it instead of eating when you aren't hungry.

Fear

Fear is a normal emotion, but many people associate it with weakness. They would rather cope with it unhealthily than say they are afraid. It might not seem like fear since it differs from anxiety, stress, or sadness, but it can also lead to compulsive eating. Any negative emotion can lead to overeating if you don't address or confront it. There is no denying that confronting our fears isn't easy, while at other times, we aren't sure what scares us exactly. For instance, are you afraid of commitment? Or are you afraid of getting hurt, so you avoid commitment?

Figuring out the relationship between your fear and eating behavior is significant. For instance, if you are afraid of gaining weight, you might go through phases of severe dieting and deprive yourself, to phases of overeating and indulging in the things you were denied. Other fears, like fear of failure, change, death, falling in love, etc., lead to compulsive eating. You could even be afraid to face your fears because you don't know whether you can conquer them. Conquering your fear isn't easy, but it is possible. You need someone to guide and motivate you, especially if you have a crippling fear. Look for a solution to help you eliminate your fear for good, but wherever it is, you will not find it in your fridge.

Anger

No one gets angry for no reason. Anger is a very powerful emotion stemming from frustration, disappointment, or pain. Sometimes, people get angry to mask their hurt feelings or hide their vulnerability. Screaming and yelling is easier than saying, "I am in pain." Some people don't know how to express their anger healthily. For instance, if you are angry after a bad breakup, it is hard to confront that your heartbreak is causing your emotions, so you turn to food as an escape. Or if you are angry with your best friend, rather than calling them and talking things out, you resort to overeating your feelings away instead. Food distracts people from the real issue behind their anger. However, it isn't a real solution and will only subdue the anger for a short time.

Compulsive eating when you are angry can make you feel worse. People often feel guilty and ashamed after overeating, so they get mad at themselves for losing control or resorting to unhealthy behaviors to cope. You overeat to numb one emotion, but it delivers a few more. You can't suppress your anger or avoid it. It is one of those emotions that gets worse when you don't address it. Rather than eating your feelings away, find the source of your anger and calmly deal with the situation or person. If this is an issue you struggle to talk about, try healthy ways to release these feelings, like boxing or journaling.

Low Self-Esteem

Negative self-talk is damaging to a person's self-esteem. It makes you beat yourself up for every little mistake you make and exercise self-blame when anything goes wrong, even if it isn't your fault. Even the most confident people can fall victim to the voice in their heads. Negative thoughts and low self-esteem lead to unhealthy coping mechanisms like compulsive eating. This unhealthy behavior does not help you cope with negative thoughts. On the contrary, it makes them worse as you end up feeling bad about yourself for indulging in this behavior.

Low self-esteem often results from focusing on the negative and ignoring the positives. Find things you love about yourself and put them front and center. Remind yourself of all your successes and accomplishments, and understand you are human, and we all make mistakes, so go easy on yourself. We know this is easier said than done. Surrounding yourself with positive people who lift you up and remind you of how amazing you are will help battle negative self-talk. You can also practice mindfulness to become aware of when these thoughts occur to understand their triggers and deal with them.

Loneliness

External and internal factors can make a person feel lonely. External factors usually result from new situations like starting a new job or moving to a new country. Instead of sitting alone at home eating, get to know the people in your new job or city or participate in activities where you can make new friends. You need someone to distract you from being lonely and help you ease into your new life. It must be a person or a pet and not pizza.

Internal loneliness is different because it has nothing to do with the lack of people in your life. You feel lonely even when you are around friends or family. It is more powerful loneliness and probably the result of something deeper you might not be aware of, like the inability to trust others or get close to people. In this case, your only friend is food, the one constant thing you can rely on in your life. However, won't it be better to find a more permanent solution? Similar to fear, you might not find a solution by yourself, but a good therapist can help you determine the root of your loneliness so that you can deal with it.

Defeat

People who struggle with their weight can reach a moment of "acceptance." They stop dieting or watching their weight and give in to their urges. This isn't acceptance, it is defeat, but you empower it by giving it a better name. It is an excuse to keep eating while pretending to accept your body and shape. While self-acceptance is encouraged and healthy, giving in to compulsive eating is admitting defeat. This feeling stems from your inability to control your food intake. However, it is temporary, and once you realize this "acceptance" has affected your weight and life, you feel guilty and ashamed.

Jealousy

Jealousy or envy can trigger overeating. Whether you are envious of someone and want what they have or jealous and afraid that your loved one will replace you for someone better, these negative feelings can trigger compulsive eating. Experiencing these emotions don't make you a bad person, as they don't always have ill intentions. They usually stem from insecurity. Expressing these feelings can be hard out of fear of judgment, or you can't admit that you are jealous of your best friend's success or afraid your partner will leave you for their co-worker. Food provides a comfort zone where there is no judgment. It allows you to forget about your insecurities briefly.

Managing Your Emotions

Various techniques can help you manage your emotions and control your responses so that you don't give in to your compulsive eating behavior or be a slave to your feelings.

Situation Modification

Situation modification is the action you take to change the impact of an emotional situation instead of avoiding it. This strategy focuses on altering external factors. In other words, you change the situation rather than how you feel about it, which impacts your emotions. There are various ways to modify the situation.

- Injecting humor effectively reduces the tension in a situation and lightens the mood. For instance, if

two friends are arguing and you feel things are
getting tense and affecting you, tell a joke to
lighten the mood and change the subject.

- Physically removing yourself from a situation
  helps lessen its emotional impact. For instance,
  you argue with a co-worker and begin to feel
  angry. Walk away from them and give yourself
  space to calm down and return later to talk
  things out.

Attentional Deployment

Attentional deployment is when a person directs their
attention toward or away from the situation to lessen its
emotional impact. You can apply two strategies here:
concentrate on the situation or distract yourself.

- **Distraction** is intentionally diverting your
  attention from the situation's emotional influence
  and focusing on something else. For instance, your
  boss gives you negative feedback on your latest
  presentation. Instead of feeling disappointed or
  mad at your boss, redirect your thoughts to
  something positive, like when your boss praises
  your work. This strategy lessens the intensity of
  the situation's emotional impact. It also helps you
  maintain control of your facial expressions as you
  remain neutral rather than showing anger or
  disappointment. It is very helpful in a professional
  environment.
- **Concentration** is turning your attention
  toward the situation's emotional aspect. If the
  situation elicits an emotional reaction, understand

why you feel this way. It will help you understand your triggers and why certain situations make you upset or angry. For instance, you were supposed to have lunch with a friend, but they canceled at the last minute. Rather than understanding that your friend probably had an emergency, you get angry and turn to food for comfort. Instead of giving in to your emotions, understand why this simple situation has driven you to anger and get to the source of the real issue.

Cognitive Reappraisal

Cognitive reappraisal involves changing how you perceive a situation to change its emotional influence. You can do various things to alter your perception.

- You can mentally and emotionally distance yourself from the situation. Perceive it from the outside without getting emotionally involved and approach it with a clear mind. For instance, your child keeps acting out no matter how often you punish them. It has caused you to feel angry and stressed. In this case, change your perception. Instead of acting like an angry parent, which causes you to become emotional, distance yourself from your emotions and change your perception. You can calmly talk to your child or see things from their point of view.
- A good sense of humor also helps you regulate your emotions and lessen the situation's intensity.

- You can also change your perception by focusing on the positive side of a situation or looking at the bigger picture.

Response Modulation

Response modulation is directly influencing your response to a situation. In other words, you actively take a role in managing your emotional response. Certain strategies can help you to achieve this:

- Having a good night's sleep reduces stress and anger. It also helps you control your emotions since lack of sleep makes you edgy and influences your temper.
- Exercising helps reduce negative emotions.
- Suppress your reactions during intense situations to prevent loss of control. For instance, if you are having an intense conversation with someone, suppress your facial expressions to remain neutral. It helps hide your anger or frustration to control your emotional reactions.

You have it in you to control your emotions and your reactions in every situation. You merely need to unlearn unhealthy behaviors and adopt better ones.

Key Takeaways

- There is a strong relationship between food and emotions
- Negative and positive emotions can lead to compulsive eating

- If you can't change your emotional response, change the situation
- Distract yourself from negative emotions by thinking positive thoughts
- Understand your triggers
- Changing your perception can positively impact your emotions
- Learn to control your emotional response by adopting healthy behavior

Now that you know how to manage your emotions, head to the next chapter and learn to manage your eating habits.

7

MANAGING YOUR EATING HABITS

"*Eating healthy food fills your body with energy and nutrients. Imagine your cells smiling back at you and saying, Thank you.'*" – Karen Salmansohn, Designer and Self-help Author

Following a healthy diet for a healthy lifestyle is essential. You're bound to damage your body if you're stuck eating junk with little to no nutrition. Breaking bad habits takes a lot of effort, time, and courage, but without it, you'll be stuck repeating the same patterns endlessly. Most stress eaters prefer excessively unhealthy junk food, putting their diet imbalance, their hormones out of control, and their bodies at risk of numerous diseases.

The importance of healthy eating has been discussed in previous chapters, but learning to manage your food hasn't been discussed yet. Most self-help books for eating disorders provide tons of tips on controlling your weight, restricting your diet, and ultimately depriving yourself of food. These techniques don't work in the long term, as discussed previously. By now, you've probably read many diet plans and ideas to help you stick to healthy food. However, transforming your lifestyle comes at a price and is not everyone's cup of tea.

To permanently change your behavior and control your binge-eating habits, you must integrate tried and tested methods to help control your cravings while directing you towards healthier food. It doesn't mean you must go on a diet or follow a strict nutrition plan. Instead, these techniques will help get your body used to healthy eating.

The 3-3-3 Rule

The 3-3-3 rule applies to mealtimes, the number of meals a day, and your meal selection. For healthy eating habits, you should keep three meals scheduled per day. Skipping a single meal is not good for your health and also paves the way for unnecessary cravings throughout the day. So, ensure you develop the habit of never skipping a meal. Your mealtimes should be three hours apart. But how will this work with only three meals a day? A good plan is to add three snacks to your food schedule. You will have consistent meals and healthy snacks throughout the day, ensuring you don't feel hungry or the need to fill yourself up with unhealthy food. You won't be attracted to untimely binging because you know when you will eat next.

Finally, your meals must be perfectly balanced with the three essential macronutrients: fat, carbohydrates, and proteins. Divide your plate into three portions to ensure you get the accurate proportion of these nutrients. The first portion should contain protein sources, another third of grains or starch, and the remaining portion of vegetables or fruits.

Protein sources include Quinoa, beans, Chia seeds, nuts, Soy, Chickpeas,and tofu. Grains include pasta, rice, bread, tortillas, and some starchy veggies. The vegetable portion can include dried or fresh fruits and vegetables cooked or raw. These guidelines are for the three major meals of the day. For the snacks, you can eat something light yet healthy, like yogurt or other options provided in other chapters.

By following the 3-3-3 rule, you get the right amount of nutrients required for a healthy diet and provide your body with enough food to keep it satisfied.

A Personal Thoughts Diary

Creating a personal thoughts diary containing different aspects of your eating habits is useful for improving your self-awareness concerning your eating habits. You'll understand your psychological and emotional relationship with food. You'll be better equipped to understand your behavior nonjudgmentally when you note the time and place of your binge eating habits. You can also include the food you ate during these episodes and what emotions you felt during and after the binge episode.

For people wondering how this is any different than counting calories, it's significantly different. You're not required to measure the food you're eating, count calories or weigh yourself for these entries. You merely need to honestly write down your emotions and psychological behavior when exhibiting compulsive eating symptoms. When dealing with an eating disorder, it becomes increasingly challenging to understand why you feel the way you do. Over time, the basic wires connecting emotional transmissions become numb and have to be kick-started to remind yourself.

Start the entry with your uncomfortable feelings or negative thoughts you've identified. Then, move forward with other detailed questions. As you add entries for each day, peruse them to determine if there's a theme to your binge eating behavior. You'll often find a specific emotion, situation, or place that triggers your eating disorder. Ask yourself questions like:

- Does my binge eating behavior happen on days I haven't eaten enough or skipped meals?
- What emotion or feeling is present most often when I start binge eating?
- Does this food disorder only get worse in certain situations?

The answers to these questions will help you pinpoint elements you must work on to improve your eating habits and stop your binge eating habits. A personal thoughts diary can also be written in a table. For example:

Date and Time: Monday, 5:30 pm
Food: A big bag of chips/Crisps
Location and Company: In the car after a long day's work
Loss of control? Yes
Thought: I hate being alone at home
Emotion: Loneliness & Tiredness

Date and Time: Saturday, 8 pm
Food: Veggie fingers with French fries
Location and Company: At a restaurant with friends
Loss of control? No
Thought: Everyone is having fried food, so can I.
Emotion: Festive/Joyful

Date and Time: Sunday, 12 am
Food: two bowls of ice-cream
Location and Company: At home alone
Loss of control? Yes
Thought: I had a fight with my parent
Emotion: Sadness/Guilt/Shame

REGAIN Control over Trigger Foods

To get your eating habits back to normal and end binge eating, regaining control over trigger foods is essential. As discussed before, trigger foods don't necessarily have to be junk food, and these are uniquely different for every person. A previous chapter mentioned identifying the trigger foods, and once you have, it's time to regain control.

Most people shy away from reintroducing their trigger foods into their lives, not knowing that this is the right technique to help them regain their power. But, before you can do that, you must first remove these trigger foods from your environment. The reintroduction process should begin a few months after you've eliminated these foods from your surroundings. Here's how you gain control of your trigger foods:

- First, bring out the list of trigger foods you've made. This list will vary from person to person, so you must create your own list instead of going along with someone else's.
- Remove the listed trigger foods from your house temporarily. When you don't find chips, ice cream, and other trigger foods within your reach, there's less chance of a binge episode. Even if you decide

to go out and buy these items, you'll have plenty of
time on the way to think about your decision.

- If you have children in the house, you don't want
  to deprive them of these food items. Get flavors
  you're less likely to eat. For instance, if you don't
  like BBQ-flavored chips, get those for the kids.
- Once you have everything under control at home,
  slowly reintroduce the trigger foods back into your
  life. From your list of trigger foods, make
  categories of least to most intense triggering food
  items.
- First, reintroduce the food items you're least
  triggered by. For instance, if you're at a party with
  snacks, you can eat a small amount. Since these
  snacks aren't at your house, there's no chance
  you'll have access to the leftovers after the party.
- Beginning with the least triggering food items
  helps if there's a relapse. You won't have to deal
  with intense trigger foods. For instance,
  reintroduce dark chocolate before milk chocolate
  to get used to healthier eating habits. Eat these
  treats when you really want to enjoy them and not
  because you're overwhelmed or stressed.
- Eat these trigger foods with close family members
  or friends you trust. Never indulge in trigger foods
  when you're alone.

More tips for reintroducing trigger foods include:

- Sit at the dining table while eating.
- Serve small portions of food on a plate. Avoid
  eating directly from the containers.
- Once the food is served, put the containers away.

- Avoid watching TV while eating.
- Pay attention to the flavor of the food and the feeling of hunger. Don't eat mindlessly.

A Food Diary

According to society's standards, food is meant to be consumed completely. We've been taught to clean our plates regardless of whether we feel hungry or not. Our parents taught us to finish our meals no matter what, which has resulted in difficulties recognizing food-related sensations. Fortunately, these teachings have changed drastically, and parents have learned to respect their children's needs.

There's nothing better than a food diary to keep track of your feelings, hunger, and fullness levels while eating. You're probably wondering how a food diary differs from a personal thoughts diary (explained before). Where a personal thoughts diary keeps track of your food habits and emotions, a food diary monitors every meal time and the intensity of hunger and fullness before and after the meal. This exercise is proven very effective in changing eating habits. For example:

Time: Saturday, 8 am
Hunger level 0-5: 4
Meal: 1 glass of orange juice and 1 slice of toast
Fullness Level? 2
Thought: I had to leave, but still hungry

Time: Saturday, 11 am
Hunger level 0-5: 5

Meal: 1 large cupcake, 1 cup of coffee and 2 servings of butter
Fullness Level? 5
Thought: I feel like I ate too much

Time: Saturday, 2 pm
Hunger level 0-5: 1
Meal: 1 hummus and betroot sandwich, 1 glass of apple juice and 4 chocolate chip cookies
Fullness Level? 5
Thought: The chocolate chip cookies were excessive

Time: Saturday, 8 pm
Hunger level 0-5: 3
Meal: 1 large bowl of pasta, steamed veggies, 2 glasses of wine and 1 low fat yogurt
Fullness Level? 5
Thought: Overindulged with the wine. Would've preferred ice cream for dessert but opted for a low-fat option.

DEAL WITH CRAVINGS

Food cravings are a typical part of our lives, and almost everyone has to deal with cravings at some point. The real problem is dealing with these cravings when they become intense and lead you toward binge eating problems. Everyone deals differently with cravings. While some people don't pay them much heed, others are completely controlled by their cravings and binge on their favorite foods. In the latter case, people blame their behavior on a lack of self-control, leading to guilt and compulsiveness to eat more.

Food cravings are usually caused by certain smells but can also be triggered by situations or people. For instance, a tough day at work might make you look for comfort in a fast-food restaurant. Even a non-stressful situation can trigger your cravings - for instance, popcorn cravings at the cinema. Certain foods are craved more frequently than others. These foods have combined fat, carbohydrates, sugar, and salt, making them irresistible, even when we're not hungry.

The first step towards dealing with your cravings is to accept that they are perfectly normal and happen to every-one. The next step is to adopt mindfulness techniques to become aware of your cravings rather than ignore them. The more you ignore or resist them, the more likely you'll give in. Food cravings typically last for about 5 minutes, which is the secret to defeating them. If you can ride the wave and get through without giving in to your cravings for 5 minutes, you won't have trouble after that. Follow these steps to get through a craving situation:

- First, identify your craving. Think or speak to yourself, "I have the craving to eat ____," and fill the gap with whatever you are craving.
- Observe the feeling. Notice the different sensations in your body when you crave food. Do you feel sensations in your stomach? Or is it your heart that wants to eat something? Are you distracted or anxious? What is your brain telling you to do?

- Once you're aware of your thoughts, emotions, and feelings, don't suppress them. Instead, accept this craving.
- Finally, pay attention to the intensity of the craving. Observe how it rises, falls, and subsides after a while. At each point, note down the intensity of the craving. For instance, "I'm craving a chocolate shake. It started as a 4, but now it's a 9."

Set Weekly Goals

Goal setting is an important part of managing your eating habits. However, you'll most likely be unsuccessful in achieving your goals without reasonable goals. Setting goals is the easy part. The more challenging part is following through. Setting goals is common when dealing with various tasks because it makes a person feel motivated while setting them and even more so after they're completed. At the end of the day, if you've completed even one goal out of the three you set for the day, you'll feel slightly accomplished and motivated to continue the next day.

For most people dealing with poor eating habits, it's difficult to set achievable goals and follow through. You could set out to steer clear of junk food or avoid high-fat foods, but it's entirely possible not to achieve these goals. So, what is the solution? After all, you can't give up on setting goals. No, that would just add to your problems. What you can do is set reasonable goals. SMART goals. These are manageable goals within the context of a healthy and happy life.

On the other hand, unrealistic expectations ultimately lead you toward failure. Failure triggers negative emotions and, finally, the compulsion to eat excessively and unhealthily. Most people set "all or nothing" goals, which essentially benefit no one. You put all the extra effort, energy, will, focus, time, and emotions into meeting unreasonable and maybe impossible standards. Any goal that results in you sacrificing self-care or ruining your self-esteem is not reasonable. For effective goal setting, here's what you should do:

- First, identify what point you're at with respect to your eating habits and food troubles.
- Establish a reasonable goal you can complete while also managing other habits.
- Next, identify a small step you can take to achieve that goal.
- Now, break this step into half, and accomplish that.
- Once you've done this, you'll gain the confidence to move toward your set goal and have the momentum to complete your tasks.

Slow Eating Techniques

Most unhealthy eating habits are developed because you eat excessively fast. Eating fast has many dangers, including choking and consuming undigested food. Slow eating is deemed important, even essential, if you want to develop healthy eating habits and manage your food intake. When you take time to chew your food, it is broken down into smaller pieces and is easier for your body to absorb. You'll get maximum nutrients extracted from your food.

Research suggests that people who eat slower eat less than people who eat quickly. Logically, this makes sense because people's perception of how much food they're consuming is often related to the time they spend eating it when it is the quantity that matters. Furthermore, slow eating ensures you're not hungry again quickly. Additionally, when you eat slowly, you savor the taste and feel of the food instead of mindlessly swallowing it. Some strategies to eat slowly include:

- Find your ideal chewing rate. It differs for everyone and can only be configured by trying it yourself. Calculate different time lengths you chew your food, and settle with the one that works best. Ideally, you should chew for about 20 to 30 seconds.
- Before you eat, set the intention to eat slowly during the meal. It will remind you of your goal.
- During the meal, take a mindful gap. Take a sip of water, switch utensils, or inhale slowly before continuing.
- You're probably highly impacted by how fast or slow the people around you eat. So, notice the speed at which everyone else is eating, and focus on your pace.
- Take smaller bites. It helps slow down your eating process and ensures you chew your food perfectly.

Keep Yourself Hydrated

Keeping yourself hydrated is essential whether you're dealing with an eating disorder or not. More often than not, people confuse thirst with hunger, leading to eating whenever they feel thirsty, which is usually a lot, as it is for everyone. However, a surprising link between dehydration and over-eating has been discovered, making it even more important for you to keep hydrated. Staying hydrated curbs your unconscious desire to keep eating and ensures your body stays healthy.

Why do we confuse thirst and hunger? It has to do with the bodily sensations felt when we're hungry or thirsty. The sharp sensations of hunger, pain, and thirst are similar because they originate from the same region in your body and are generated by histamines. The best way to tackle this is to drink plenty of water throughout the day. This way, you won't feel thirsty as often and won't have the urge to eat something to quell your thirst.

Most people consider a dry mouth as a sign to drink water. However, they're already at a high dehydration level at this stage. Therefore, whether your mouth feels dry or not, it's important to drink water. Moreover, drinking water after eating is not as effective as drinking some before you eat. It helps in two ways: First, you'll feel full earlier because the water you drink takes up space in your stomach, leading to eating less. Second, your body requires plenty of free water to digest solid food properly. So, if you ensure your water intake is satisfactory, you'll have less trouble managing your eating habits.

What Not to Do:

Numerous tips are available online and sometimes handed out freely by people with no idea of how overeating can be managed. So, it's okay to get confused when looking for solutions that work for you. However, there is some advice you should never take concerning food management and weight loss. These include:

- Don't skip a meal or fast to manage your eating habits or lose weight.
- Don't exercise excessively; instead, stick with a mild routine. This routine isn't supposed to burn calories but instead help you improve your lifestyle.
- Don't detox or go on cleansing diets.
- Don't under-eat during the day because this will only lead to overeating at night.
- Finally, don't suffer in silence. Speak to someone if you feel you can't manage everything on your own.

Key Takeaways

- Respect the 3-3-3 rule to manage better your eating habits; 3 meals and 3 snacks every 3 hours.
- To keep track of your binge-eating habits and associated thoughts, keep a personal thoughts diary and check your progress regularly.
- For some people, specific foods, typically with high sugar and fat, can be triggering. The list varies from person to person but almost always leads to a compulsive eating episode.
- Avoiding these trigger foods can be advantageous in the short term but hurt you in the long term. It's better to reintroduce trigger foods gradually into your life.
- Intuitively eating is key to gaining control over your eating habits and rediscovering the pleasure of eating.

- It's important to consider your hungriness and fullness levels when planning to eat to improve your food habits.
- Keeping a food diary is a great idea to note these sensations and build awareness effectively.
- Dealing with cravings doesn't need to be difficult and only requires time and effort.
- Slow eating techniques can help reduce your total intake and help with stressful eating situations.

Once you've learned to effectively manage your eating habits better, the next step is to discover how to manage stressful situations without falling prey to a binge eating episode. Learning food management techniques will be useless without actively trying to reduce stressful situations. So, turn the page to the next chapter, and discover how you can cope with stressful situations that often lead to compulsive eating habits.

8

STRESS SOLUTIONS

"*Even if you are in strong recovery, major life stressors or transitions may make you more vulnerable to eating disorder thoughts. It's during these times when good self-care, healthy coping tools, and getting support is especially important. Take care of yourself.*"— Beth Pilcher, LISW-CP

Stress is an inevitable part of life; it can manifest as minor annoyances or major emergencies. You might not be able to alter the stressful circumstance, but you can control your response. Stress eating is a dangerous way to deal with stress.

Doing what is right rather than what is convenient with mental health and other important aspects of human life is critical. Therefore, knowing and understanding effective stress-relieving strategies to soothe your body and mind during and after stressful episodes is crucial.

No general rule exists for effective stress management because what works for you might not work for someone else. So, you should have various stress-reduction techniques on hand.

There are four major categories of stress solutions. As you read on, consider the stress-relieving techniques you could use at home, at work, or in the midst of a conflict.

Short-Term Stress Solutions

These are quick-relief techniques that can be used at any time. They're free and provide immediate relief. However, these stress-relief strategies might not provide long-term relief. It is essential to know these techniques to implement them when you feel stressed.

The following are some short-term stress solutions:

Guided Imagery

Guided imagery is similar to taking a mental vacation. It is envisioning yourself in your happy place, like sitting on a beach, appreciating the sound of the waves, the scent of the water, and the warmth of the sand beneath your feet.

You can use guided imagery to alleviate stress by listening to an audio recording of someone guiding you through a peaceful scene while closing your eyes. These are available from professional websites on the internet.

You can also do guided visualization exercises on your own. Close your eyes for a moment and imagine yourself in a peaceful setting. Visualize all the calming sensations, and when you feel relaxed open your eyes.

Meditation

Meditation offers immediate and long-term benefits for stress management. You can practice numerous meditation techniques; each is distinct and appealing.

Create a catchphrase to repeat as you breathe deeply. Alternatively, spend a brief period practicing mindfulness, which entails being in the present moment. If you are focused on the present moment, you cannot dwell on the past or be concerned about the future.

Mindfulness and meditation can significantly reduce your overall stress levels by bringing you back to the present moment. However, they require practice.

Mindfulness

The term "mindfulness" means focusing on the present. Mindfulness and mindfulness-based cognitive therapy (MBCT), a subtype of cognitive behavioral therapy, are awareness-based stress-reduction techniques.

Consistently meditating, even for short periods, improve your mood and reduce stress and worry. Numerous books, apps, and websites can teach mindfulness basics; if you want to try it, look for MBCT-focused therapists in your neighborhood.

Progressive Muscle Relaxation

Progressive muscle relaxation is relaxing each group of muscles one at a time. You might be wondering, "How do I do this?" How do I know if my muscles are relaxed?

First, take a few slow, deep breaths. Then, focus on contracting and relaxing each muscle, beginning with your forehead and working your way down to your toes. When you contract your muscles, you feel more tense and stiff, but when you relax, your body goes into a calm state.

With practice, you will become more adept at identifying muscular tension and tightness and relax more quickly. However, each time you practice, you should experience a wave of serenity.

Deep Breathing

Simply paying attention to or changing how you breathe can reduce stress. Only a few minutes of breathing exercises can help you relax your entire body and mind. The good news is no one will see you performing them. Consequently, whether you're in a meeting or seated in a crowded theater, breathing exercises could reduce stress.

To practice deep breathing, fill your abdomen with air as you inhale deeply through your nose. Hold your breath for one second, then exhale gently through your nose while counting to three. As you exhale, visualize yourself releasing all of your tension and stress.

Nature Time

More time spent outdoors helps reduce stress. Spending as little as 10 minutes in a natural environment improves physiological markers of mental well-being, such as perceived stress and happiness in college-aged individuals.

Visit local parks and arboretums more frequently. You could also go for a walk and enjoy the scenery. Walking is a simple yet effective way to refresh your mind and body, whether you need a break from a tedious assignment or want to enjoy a stroll after work. It enables you to shift your perspective while providing health benefits.

Physical Touch

Human contact can have a calming effect and enhance your ability to deal with stress. Physical touch, like hugging, cuddling, sex, etc., can greatly reduce stress. Sex and pleasant physical interaction can alleviate loneliness and stress. Hugging a loved one has several benefits. Oxytocin, a hormone commonly released during a hug or cuddle, has been linked to higher happiness and lower stress levels.

When stressed, you might notice physical symptoms, such as increased heart rate and high blood pressure. The hormone oxytocin, released when you hug a loved one, helps to lower blood pressure and heart rate.

Physical touch also reduces the cortisol levels and norepinephrine in your body, which are stress hormones. Don't be afraid to ask a loved one for a hug when you're stressed.

Aromatherapy

Aromatherapy uses scents to improve mood and overall health. Using aromatherapy to alleviate stress can help you feel more energized and relaxed. Some scents influence brain wave activity and lower stress hormone levels in the body.

Consider candles, diffusers, or body products for aromatherapy. Lavender, geranium, vetiver, rose, neroli, bergamot, ylang-ylang, sandalwood, orange blossom, Roman chamomile, frankincense, and others can relieve stress and enhance your mood.

Hobbies and Artwork

Making time for things you enjoy is a healthy way to relieve stress; engage in pleasurable activities daily. It is worthwhile to devote 15 to 20 minutes daily as preventative stress measures. Reading, needlework, creating art, playing golf, watching movies, solving puzzles, playing cards, etc., are relaxing activities.

It might have been easy to tap into your creative side when you were younger, but if you've lost touch with your appreciation for art, reconnect with it again. Consider using a coloring book if you dislike painting or drawing. Adult coloring books are becoming increasingly popular, and for valid reasons, as coloring is a great way to unwind.

Long-Term Stress Solutions

What long-term actions can you take to reduce mental stress? Some behaviors help boost stress resistance and overall wellness. For example, those who regularly meditate or exercise are less worried when confronted with a difficult problem. Consequently, it's critical to cultivate a way of life allowing you to deal with stress and overcome obstacles healthily.

Some long-term stress solutions are as follows:

Consume a Healthy Diet

A well-balanced diet is essential for long-term stress management. Stress eating and grabbing high-fat or sugar meals will temporarily relieve your tension but negatively impact your overall health in the long run. A poor diet increases your susceptibility to stress, causing health problems such as increased blood sugar and cholesterol. Foods like eggs, avocados, and walnuts help with mood management and energy balance.

Consume Stress Relief Supplements

Several vitamins and minerals significantly impact your body's stress response and mood regulation. A lack of vitamins could affect your mental health and ability to cope with stress. Certain nutritional supplements can help reduce stress and improve your mood.

Consuming sufficient minerals and vitamins daily to enhance your body's response to stress is essential. They include the following:

- L-theanine: Research has shown that this amino acid aids stress management, relaxation, and improved sleep.
- Melatonin: This natural hormone regulates your body's circadian rhythm. When the quality of your sleep improves, you will feel less stressed.
- B vitamins: These multivitamins help reduce stress, improve mood, and lower homocysteine levels.
- Ashwagandha: This plant helps boost the body's resistance to physical and mental stress.

However, not everyone will benefit from or feel safe using dietary supplements. If you want to use supplements to reduce stress, first consult a doctor.

Schedule Recreational Activities

Leisure activities are an excellent way to unwind. Many believe that because their lives are so hectic, they do not have time for extracurricular activities. However, scheduling leisure activities could be critical to feeling your best at all times.

In addition, you will perform more effectively when you feel better, so taking a break from work could increase your productivity. Hobbies and leisure activities, whether quilting or gardening, are essential for living the best life possible.

Practice Self-Talk and Affirmations

How you speak to yourself is important. Self-doubt and harsh self-criticism contribute to mental stress. You will become stressed if you are preoccupied with thoughts like "I am not good enough" and "I can't bear this." It is essential to have a more realistic and empathic internal dialogue.

Compassionate internal dialogue helps deal with your negative self-talk and self-doubt. Positive affirmations will help you develop a more positive mindset. Sympathetic dialogue helps you control your emotions and take proactive measures.

Participate in Yoga

Yoga has gained popularity among people of all ages as an exercise and stress relief. There are numerous yoga styles, but they all aim to unite the body and mind by enhancing body and breath awareness.

It incorporates controlled breathing, physical movement, meditation, and moderate exercise, which are effective stress relievers. While a single yoga session could positively affect you immediately, consistent yoga practice is more likely to have a long-term positive impact.

Yoga helps with stress management and the symptoms of anxiety and depression. It can also help with psychological health. These benefits are related to how your nervous system and stress response are affected. Yoga increases gamma-aminobutyric acid levels in your body, a neurotransmitter deficient in people with mood disorders.

Yoga has numerous health benefits for the body, mind, and soul. Take a class, enroll in an online course, or use an app to get started.

Maintain a Grateful Attitude

Gratitude helps you recognize your blessings. Consider all the wonderful things in your life, such as a beautiful day or a safe commute to work. Gratitude can be very empowering because it makes you aware of the resources available to manage your stress.

Grateful individuals have better mental health, less stress, and a higher quality of life. Make gratitude a habit by writing down five things you are thankful for each day in a gratitude journal, or make it a family tradition to express gratitude at the dinner table.

Exercise Regularly

Physical activity is essential for stress reduction and mental health enhancement. The good news is there are numerous physical activities you can engage in to reduce stress. Walking, joining a gym, strength training, fishing, hiking, aerobic or spin classes, and other activities can help relieve stress.

Practice Self-Care

Making time for self-care will aid in stress reduction. Stress and burnout are associated with a lack of self-care. People who practice self-care have lower stress levels and a higher quality of life.

Setting aside time for yourself is essential to living a healthy life. Self-care does not have to be complicated or time-consuming. It merely means being concerned with your happiness and well-being.

Try Biofeedback

This behavioral technique teaches you how to manage stress by monitoring your heart rate, muscle tension, and other vital signs as you relax. It is used to regain control of certain biological processes causing stress and discomfort.

Biofeedback can help you understand how your body responds to stress and manage it better. Various individuals use biofeedback to stop attacks or headaches like migraines. You can get more information from your healthcare provider.

Create a Zen Area

Designate a stress-free zone around your home or office where you can unwind anytime. When tension rises, set up a comfortable chair or burn incense and spend some time there.

Eliminate Caffeine and Nicotine from Your Diet

Those using nicotine often describe it as a stress reliever. However, nicotine increases stress by raising physical arousal and decreasing blood flow and respiration. Smoking won't help with ongoing stress or body pains because it can exacerbate painful symptoms.

Caffeine in coffee, tea, chocolate, and energy drinks, stimulates your central nervous system. Excessive consumption can aggravate and heighten anxiety symptoms.

Furthermore, excessive use could impair your ability to sleep, resulting in stress and anxiety. If caffeine makes you jittery or anxious, consider substituting it with decaffeinated herbal tea or water. Each person has a different maximum caffeine tolerance.

Consider your tolerance because caffeine-sensitive individuals might experience increased anxiety and tension after consuming significantly less caffeine in their diet.

Problem-Oriented Stress Solution

Most stress treatments focus on changing your emotions. However, changing your environment can sometimes make you feel better – it is known as problem-focused coping, as opposed to emotion-focused coping. Problem-focused coping is taking action to eliminate the stressor rather than changing your feelings about the stressor. They include:

Examine Your To-Do Lists

If you attempt to finish 20 hours of work in 16 hours, you will experience stress. Reduce your workload, and it will be easier to get through the day feeling better.

It might necessitate quitting a committee or hiring a personal assistant. By improving your time management skills, you can reduce your stress levels.

Set Some Boundaries for Yourself

Not all external pressures are beyond your control. Over-commitment can result in increased stress and less time for self-care. Control of your personal life will relieve stress and protect your mental health.

One strategy for achieving this goal could be to say 'no' more frequently. Remember, if you frequently take on more than you can handle, juggling multiple responsibilities can make you feel overwhelmed.

Furthermore, establishing boundaries is a smart way to protect your well-being, especially with those who increase your stress levels. Asking a friend or relative not to drop by unexpectedly or canceling plans with a friend who stirs up trouble will do the trick.

Don't Put Things off Any Longer

Another way to deal with stress is to keep track of your priorities and avoid procrastination. When you procrastinate, your productivity suffers, leaving you with little time to handle responsibilities. It will affect your health and ability to sleep.

A Chinese study of 140 medical students found a link between procrastination and elevated stress levels.

If you frequently procrastinate, developing the habit of making a prioritized to-do list is beneficial. Set realistic deadlines and work your way through the list. Give yourself uninterrupted time to complete assigned tasks. In contrast, multitasking can be stressful.

Talk to a Friend

Getting emotional support and friendship is vital. When something bothers you, expressing your feelings to a friend can be helpful. The key to stress management is surrounding yourself with optimistic people.

Confiding with a relative or friend gives you the social support you require. Furthermore, you need to expand your social circle. If you don't have supportive friends, join a group, attend a support meeting, or see a professional.

Eliminate Stress-Inducing Activities

Eliminate the stressors in your life to feel more at ease. Constantly watching the news and consuming alcohol increases your stress levels. Smartphones, computers, and tablets are integral to many people's daily lives. While these devices are frequently required, excessive use can cause stress.

Excessive screen time is associated with decreased psychological well-being and increased stress in adults and children. Additionally, excessive screen time impairs your ability to sleep, raising your stress level. Make a few adjustments to your daily routine to avoid being constantly stressed.

Examine and Adhere to Your Principles

Regardless of your hectic life, the more you align your actions with your convictions, the better you will feel. Consider your values before engaging in any activity or commenting on a situation. Also, in light of the demanding expectations and obligations you face daily, engage in activities consistent with your values and resonate with you personally.

Rapid Response Stress Solution

These include practical tips for reducing stress and tension. Among them are:

Don't Be Too Hard on Yourself

Recognize that no matter how hard you try, you will not accomplish everything perfectly. Also, learn to accept the aspects of your life you cannot control.

Counting Back

When your anxieties are out of control, count from one to ten and then back to relax. It is difficult to be anxious about an upcoming exam or job interview when you are preoccupied with remembering the number that comes before seven.

Stretch Yourself

Standing up to stretch your muscles can help you relax during a demanding task. Try chest-opening stretches or shoulder rolls.

Shut Your Eyes

Simply closing your eyes will give you a break from work or home. It's a simple technique for calming yourself and regaining your composure.

Squeeze a Stress Ball

Squeeze a stress ball when you feel like hitting a colleague or roommate. It is a quick, portable, and nonviolent means of relieving stress.

Laugh and Be Happy

There is science behind the laughter, despite it appearing as an absurd method of relieving stress. Laughing improves blood circulation and boosts the immune system. Never lose your sense of humor when stressed or in a difficult situation. Laughter greatly aids relaxation.

Apply Cold Water to Your Wrists

When stressed, go to the bathroom and spray cold water behind your earlobes and on your wrists. Since vital arteries are beneath your epidermis, cooling these areas helps your body relax.

Keep a Record

Putting your emotions on paper makes them less frightening. Try journaling before a major exam to help you relax.

Slurp Some Honey

Drink some honey to alleviate your stress. It contains ingredients that reduce inflammation in the brain, making it a natural antibacterial, skin moisturizer, and antidepressant.

Get Yourself Organized

A lack of organization could exacerbate your anxiety. At the office, declutter your desk and only place essential items on it.

Key Takeaways

The four major categories of stress solutions are as follows:

1. **Short-Term Stress Solutions**

- Guided Imagery
- Meditation
- Mindfulness
- Progressive Muscle Relaxation
- Deep Breathing
- Nature Time
- Physical Touch
- Aromatherapy
- Hobbies and Artwork

1. **Long-Term Stress Solutions**

- Consume a Healthy Diet
- Consume Stress Relief Supplements
- Schedule Recreational Activities
- Practice Self-talk and Affirmations
- Participate in Yoga
- Maintain a Grateful Attitude
- Exercise and Physical Activity
- Practice Self-Care
- Try Biofeedback
- Make a Zen Area
- Eliminate Caffeine and Nicotine from Your Diet

1. **Problem-Oriented Stress Solution**

- Examine your TO-DO lists.
- Set Limits and Practice saying no
- Learn to Stop Delaying Tasks
- Talk with a Friend
- Eliminate the Stress-Adding Activities
- Examine Your Principles and Adhere to them

1. **Rapid Response Stress Solution**

- Don't Be Too Hard on Yourself
- Counting Back
- Stretch Yourself
- Shut Your Eyes
- Squeeze a Stress Ball
- Laugh and Be Happy
- Apply Cold Water to Your Wrist
- Keep a Record of It
- Slurp Some Honey
- Get Yourself Organized

Although stress is an unavoidable part of life, it is harmful to your physical and emotional health if it persists. Fortunately, several techniques can assist you in reducing stress and improving your overall psychological health. Exercise, mindfulness, yoga practice, spending more time outdoors, etc., are effective strategies. Choose the best method for you from the tips above, and start your journey back to wholeness.

You've read about the triggers and solutions for stress eating. The final chapter explores techniques and strategies to avoid these triggers.

9

AVOIDING A FUTURE RELAPSE

"*Don't stay too long in the shame-filled grounds of relapse. Fertile soil awaits your return and your recovery.*"-Holli Kenley; Mountain Air: Relapsing and Finding the Way Back, One Breath at a Time

Good for you if you're feeling inspired to combat your stress eating as you worked through the previous chapters. Discovering a new lifestyle change from emotional eating means you are extra careful not to get triggered again. Sometimes though, things don't always go as planned.

We all have bad days now and again, but with emotional eating relapse creeping up on you so often, do you feel like you keep hitting the same roadblocks? You know emotional eating is a problem, and you understand why you're doing it. But when things get tough, all those stressors and pressures come rushing back with a vengeance. If there's one issue that is constantly present in most people, it's stress. So, how do you avoid an emotional eating relapse? Read on for tips and strategies to avoid an emotional eating relapse.

Relapse: What It Is and Why It Happens

When you first recover from emotional eating, you're filled with hope and think it will be different this time. You know what triggered your last binge. You understand why you did it. You have new tools to avoid a relapse, and now the recovery process will be different because you'll remember those red alert moments and won't fall off the wagon again. Except, life doesn't work like that. Does it? Recovery isn't as straightforward as we would like to believe.

Despite our best intentions and efforts to eliminate binge eating from our lives, it often returns at some point, usually when we least expect it. Of all the negative habits we develop while recovering from stress eating, eating seems the easiest one to break; after all, what's more, natural than hunger? So, why does this keep reoccurring? Why does something so simple sneak up on us time and time again? Read on to learn more about what a relapse means and how to prevent it from happening again.

What Is Relapse?

A relapse is a re-occurrence of emotional eating where someone has been recovering well. Suddenly and unexpectedly, they have a large amount of food in one sitting. It can happen if you're unsure of being hungry but consume a large amount of food anyway. Relapse can happen during the initial recovery stages or after years of being free from bingeing. People who struggle with eating for a long time can experience a "stepped" relapse, gradually consuming more food in one sitting over several days, weeks, or even months, before suddenly "stepping" back into a full-blown binge.

Why Do We Relapse?

As we know, overeating is a way of feeling more in control of our emotions and life and is often a response to a trigger, something that happened or happening in your life. When you have an addiction, any failure or slips along the way feel like a complete crash and burn. After all, one stumble is all it takes to trigger a downward spiral of self-loathing and shame, triggering another relapse. But what are the reasons behind relapse? If you know what triggers your compulsive eating, you can better prevent it from happening again. As with most addictions, the reasons behind relapse vary depending on the person. However, there are various common triggers many people experience after treatment:

- You're feeling unwell - If you're experiencing a health issue, like a cold or flu, your body's natural hunger cues might be altered. It could make it difficult to distinguish between a relapse, and you're just not feeling well. If this happens, be kind to yourself and don't punish yourself for not knowing the difference. Let your eating remain relaxed and get some rest to help you feel better
- You've slipped into old habits - If you're not vigilant about monitoring your eating habits and not getting enough support from others, you could fall back into old habits. If you notice this happening, recognizing it early before it becomes a full-blown relapse is important.

- Something triggered you - It could be a particular memory or situation brought on by a change in your life, such as a move, losing a loved one, getting married, divorced, or having a child.

Ultimately, stress eating is a coping mechanism to calm yourself down when emotions are running high. Unfortunately, as with many of our eating disordered behaviors, it does not solve the problem. It makes it worse. The more you engage, the more you become conditioned to rely on it. The more you rely on it, the more likely you will have a relapse, especially if you're not attentive to your emotional state.

Don't Beat Yourself Up

Recognizing a relapse has happened and that you do not beat yourself up over it is crucial. As discussed, relapsing often means we need more support and encouragement. Emotional eating is a difficult behavior to give up, and many people struggle with it for years before they succeed. Don't shut yourself out from others and isolate yourself out of shame, guilt, and self-blame. Instead, speak to someone about what's happened and ask for help. Be kind and forgiving to yourself. Remember, you're human, and it's okay to make mistakes.

How to Prevent Relapse: The Best Strategies to Keep It from Happening

You know how difficult it can be to break the cycle of unhealthy eating habits. If you're ready to take your recovery to the next level, learning to prevent relapse is a great step in the right direction. Worsening your eating habits is like digging yourself into a hole that becomes increasingly difficult to get out of. The more often you give in to unhealthy cravings and binge eating impulses, the harder it becomes not to do so again. It's an insidious pattern many people struggle with for years before finally breaking through and establishing new, healthier habits. However, recognizing you are at risk for relapse and taking specific steps beforehand increases your chances of avoiding it in the future significantly. These strategies have helped many with their struggles, so they can help you, too.

Talk to Someone You Trust

You might have tried to handle your binge eating on your own and failed, or perhaps you wanted to see if there's another way to get past it. In any case, talking to a friend or family member you trust is a great first step toward regaining control and ending binge eating. Well-meaning people will offer support and encouragement, but finding someone who offers an objective perspective is important. Keeping your struggles to yourself is dangerous, especially if you are experiencing intense cravings, making you want to binge eat. Whether you decide to confide in a close friend, family member, or therapist, choosing someone you trust and feel comfortable opening up to is crucial. Your partner might provide the support and insight you need, but you must ensure they are open to the conversation.

Learn What Your Triggers Are

It might sound simple, but you'll never stop if you don't know why you're stress eating. It's essential to figure out what is causing you to binge eat so that you can make the proper adjustments to avoid future binges. Over-eating isn't merely mindless munching; it's a coping mechanism. You could be using food to make yourself feel better about something or to fill an emotional void. If you don't know what it is you're trying to fix with your binges, it's impossible to stop it from happening again.

Distract Yourself

Distractions are powerful tools to help you avoid thinking about food and what triggers cravings, including stress and boredom. When stressed, distracted by work, or otherwise preoccupied, it's much harder to connect your stress and overeating. Distractions help keep you from falling into a vicious cycle of eating when you're stressed and becoming increasingly upset and depressed when you can't eat. Distracting yourself from hobbies, activities, or friends will minimize cravings. People with strong social support often feel being around others helps alleviate their loneliness or isolation. However, being distracted by distractions doesn't mean you should run away from your problems. You must face them to control and prevent them from controlling you.

Don't Tempt Yourself with Trigger Foods

Food is meant to nourish your body, not make you sick or addicted. Unfortunately, many people turn to junk food when stressed, depressed, or need an emotional boost. These foods are often high in sugar and fat, which can exacerbate your cravings by triggering your dopamine receptors. Don't let your cravings lead you down a path of self-destruction. If you're having a hard time resisting unhealthy cravings, don't keep unhealthy foods in your house. If you know, you'll be stressed or need an extra boost during the day, keep healthy snacks on hand you know won't send you into a binge-eating frenzy.

Plan Ahead

Preparing your meals in advance makes you less likely to be tempted by high-calorie snacks. You'll also have more time to eat healthy meals that keep you full until bedtime.

While meal prep is ideal, it can be challenging to maintain over the long term. Here are some tips to help take the pressure off:

- Create a weekly meal plan. It will help you to stay on track and ensure your diet is balanced
- Shop for ingredients in advance. It allows you to stock up on the foods you need most, so you don't have to run out at the last minute
- Plan for leftovers. You can enjoy a healthy snack or meal without worrying about what to eat next.
- Go shopping for delicious cooking recipes. This will get you excited about trying new meals. Plus, according to researchers in The Journal of Positive Psychology (2016), cooking is a natural stress reliever.

Don't Diet

One of the main reasons people binge when they diet is because they feel deprived. When we feel deprived, our eating gets out of control. Remember, not dieting will not cause you to binge. Instead, it increases your risk of relapse. So, if you want to avoid a stress eating relapse, do not diet. However, if you want to diet, following a healthy diet plan that includes whole grains, lean proteins, and plenty of fruits and vegetables is vital.

Find Healthy Ways to Manage (With Therapy)

If you feel you're really struggling, there is no shame in seeking professional help. Talking with someone about your struggles with emotional eating and getting the support necessary to overcome this problem is important. A professional will help you recognize the signs of relapse before you make another poor food choice that could set you back. It might be difficult to fight the urge to eat unhealthy foods due to emotional triggers if you're going through a stressful period or dealing with a mental illness like depression. But even when you feel you can control yourself, take the time to track your food intake and stay vigilant about your eating habits. If you see yourself slipping into old patterns, it's time to seek professional help.

Eat Breakfast

Despite the phrase being a tad cliché, it is true that breakfast is one of the most important meals of the day. It provides a nutritious start giving your body the energy to function. Food cravings are often due to a lack of nutrients in your system, which can be caused by skipping breakfast or not eating enough throughout the day. A healthy breakfast will help prevent overeating later in the day by keeping you full and satisfied.

When choosing what to eat for breakfast, remember variety is key. Use different foods every day, like oatmeal with fruit and almond milk, Greek yogurt with granola, and scrambled eggs with spinach and tomatoes.

Also, don't forget to include protein in every meal. Protein helps regulate our blood sugar levels, which helps prevent cravings throughout the day.

Identify the Reasons for the Urge to Eat

Overeating is a complex phenomenon influenced by many different factors. The key to successful relapse prevention is identifying the underlying causes of your overeating so that you can take steps to address them. Using the advice outlined in this book to identify the reasons for overeating helps you avoid a binge eating relapse and develop healthier habits. Remember, the most common causes of emotional eating are:

- Stressful life events, like relationship problems, financial difficulties, or family illness, can lead to emotional eating
- Another common cause of overeating is boredom. People who feel bored eat because they feel it provides an escape from their current situation
- Finally, people overeat when they lack self-control due to a lack of willpower or poor decision-making skills.

Use the HALT Model

The HALT method is great for those with trouble identifying the causes of overeating. HALT stands for Hungry, Angry, Lonely, or Tired, the four main feelings that lead to relapse. These principles were developed to help people make better decisions about their drinking and other drug use, especially when tempted to go back to using. It is now used by anyone with addictive tendencies, especially those with stress eating.

You can use it when feeling the urge to eat. When the urge is too strong to suppress, take a moment and HALT. Ask yourself if you feel hungry, angry, lonely, or tired. It will make you more aware of your feelings and help identify the causes.

Hunger can be an emotional or physical need. Physical hunger is easily dealt with (make sure you eat a healthy breakfast and load up on vegetables), but emotional hunger is more difficult to identify. It could be the need for affection, achievement, or awareness.

Angry feelings are healthy emotions everyone experiences from time to time. To express your anger appropriately, you must HALT and determine the reason. It could be another person, situation, or even you.

Loneliness is mostly caused by a lack of social connections. HALT and ask yourself if you feel disconnected from your friends, family, or community. Loneliness can also result from feeling overwhelmed and overburdened by responsibilities like work or school, personal problems like illness or divorce, or being stuck in a rut. Loneliness is not always bad; it can be good in certain circumstances. For example, loneliness can help you feel more secure and content when you're away from people. If you feel lonely, talk to someone about it. It might just be that simple. If it's a persistent feeling, consider joining a local group related to your hobbies, or look for adult-specific meetings in your area.

Tired comes from lack of sleep or too much stress. When we are tired, our mind is less attentive. We naturally tend to be less in the present moment and dwell on the past or future, making us anxious and irritable. The best way to combat tiredness is to take regular breaks from your computer and phone to relax and recharge. Also, stay active when you're feeling tired by taking a walk or going for a run. If you're becoming short-tempered while you're tired, take a break from whatever makes you angry. It's natural to get tired sometimes, but ensure it does not affect your happiness.

Embrace Your Emotions

When you binge eat, the first thing to understand is it isn't about hunger. It's an emotional response that happens when stressed, depressed, or anxious. It can happen anytime and for many reasons. But when you have an emotional trigger, it's important to know how to recognize it and keep from bingeing.

One way is by embracing emotion. When stressed, sit with the feeling fully instead of pushing it away. You'll realize the desire decreases, and the anxiety will subside after a few minutes. This action is very different from avoiding the feeling and giving yourself short bursts of relief. Being present with your emotions is a powerful way to reduce their intensity and learn to ride them out before they over-whelm you, so you don't need to binge.

Find Your Happy Place

A happy place is anywhere you feel comfortable and calm – your couch, bed, or in the car, if that is where you eat after work. Whatever it is, find an environment where you can be at peace and enjoy yourself no matter what. It could be as simple as setting out a small plate of healthy snacks or making a cup of tea. You might also take a hot bath or shower before feeling the urge to binge. For the time being, at least until you feel you make some leeway, avoid going out to eat as much as possible. The less time you spend with people who might tempt you to overeat, the more likely you will stay at home and eat instead. Once you've found your happy place, ensure to return there whenever you feel the urge to binge. Eventually, this habit will become so ingrained that the desire to retreat to your happy place will be more powerful than your desire for comfort foods.

Set Healthy Boundaries

One common cause of binge eating is trying to please everyone around you. If your job or family members are stressing you, or you put too much pressure on yourself to be perfect, you might be emotionally eating to escape those feelings. If you binge eat out of frustration, anger, or exhaustion, you know how easy it is to fall back into unhealthy habits when you're overwhelmed. Learning to set healthy boundaries is one of the best ways to combat this habit. Don't let other people's expectations weigh you down and trigger your cravings. If someone is getting on your nerves, or you're overwhelmed with work, take a step back and regain control over your emotions.

Start Setting Smaller, More Achievable Goals

Only you can prevent a relapse. Setting smaller, more manageable goals can make your journey less painful and more effective. Set treatment goals. They are smaller, achievable goals to track your progress over time. Instead of trying to "overcome" your emotional eating, focus on smaller, more concrete goals like reducing the frequency of your binges, exercising more often, or taking better care of yourself.

Commit to a Fitness Routine

Working out is more than just a good way to burn calories and stay in shape. It is an excellent way to manage cravings, relieve stress, and keep your mind healthy. If you struggle with over-eating, it's important to care for yourself physically and mentally. You might be experiencing intense cravings, making you want to binge eat, or experiencing a lot of stress in your life. Working out will help you stay in control of your emotions and cravings and improve your mood and self-esteem. Find an exercise you enjoy and can do regularly, like walking, yoga, jogging, or swimming.

Stay Positive

When you're positive about your treatment, that optimism will help you maintain your motivation and keep you from feeling defeated. Besides, it makes the process much more enjoyable. Being positive also helps build your tolerance for certain comfort foods because you realize that no food can truly make you happy. Only you can do that. As a result, being positive helps you accept that some days will be better than others. Remember, even if you feel positive, it doesn't mean you are cured. It's a slow process and takes time. You can only control what you do, so try your best to stay as positive as possible.

Be Kind to Yourself

Finally, the most important thing you can do to avoid relapse is to be kind to yourself. It's easy to get frustrated and impatient with your progress, especially when overcoming an eating disorder. Emotional eating is a chronic condition and is difficult to overcome. You might not be able to prevent every binge, but you can significantly reduce the frequency of your binges and work toward a full recovery. Remember, you don't have to overcome this alone.

Key Takeaway

- While relapsing is painful, it is a part of the process
- The more you rely on emotional eating, the more likely you will relapse, especially if you're not attentive to your emotional state
- It's normal to have days when you go overboard with food, but that doesn't mean you can't stop it from happening again
- There are many strategies to keep binge eating from reoccurring
- The best way is to understand why it happened in the first place and work on resolving those issues within yourself as soon as possible.

AFTERWORD

The truth is that stress doesn't come from your boss, your kids, your spouse, traffic jams, health challenges, or other circumstances. It comes from your thoughts about your circumstances. – Andrew Bernstein

Stress eating, like substance and alcohol use, is a temporary solution that does nothing to alleviate stress. A healthier approach is accepting the reality of stress and bad moods and developing more effective coping mechanisms.

There is a difference between a good negative feeling that helps us figure out how to deal with a challenging situation by learning to tolerate it and a harmful negative feeling that does not help us to resolve the problem; instead, it adds to our distress.

While some individuals actively reward themselves with a packet of chips at the end of a rough day, others unknowingly engage in stress eating. The human mind goes into automatic mode. It gets ingrained in our daily routines, and we don't even notice it's happening.

Recognizing the distinction between physical and stress hunger will help you avoid mindless eating. Assess your emotional and physiological state before diving into that box of chocolates. Each person experiences hunger uniquely, but common bodily indications include a rumbling or empty belly, a lack of energy, and even a headache. If you have a hunger for food but none of these symptoms, it's possible you're searching for solace or something to take your mind off things.

If you're not really hungry but are eating out of habit or to relieve stress, you should reconsider your method.

Whenever you are in the thick of a difficult event, any positive diversion, like strolling, getting some fresh air, completing a minute of mindfulness meditation, or contacting a buddy, might help you resist the urge to go for unhealthy food. Water consumption is also helpful since thirst is sometimes misunderstood as hunger.

In the long run, identifying and addressing the source of your stress will benefit you more than restraining your eating urges. Sustainable ways to deal with stress include working out, getting enough sleep, and eating well. If you have persistent problems with stress eating, it will be beneficial to consult with a specialist to assist you in identifying and resolving the underlying problems contributing to your behavior.

Before your emotions grow so intense, you can no longer think rationally, giving them the attention they require is crucial. Emotional eating occurs when an emotional demand goes unsatisfied.

However, it's also crucial to recognize that your feelings will sometimes win, and punishing yourself for sometimes stress eating will only make things worse.

Unfortunately, we place a lot of importance on what we eat, and the remorse associated with more decadent options adds unnecessary pressure to our already stressful lives. In the long run, your success depends on whether or not you can maintain a healthy eating habit and diet.

Put into practice all you've learned in this book.

Thank you for accompanying me on this adventure. Remember, taking a moment to breathe before giving in to your hunger is a huge step in the right direction.

BIBLIOGRAPHY

Nicole Galan, R. N. (2018, February 15). Emotional eating: How to overcome stress eating. Medicalnewstoday.com. https://www.medical-newstoday.com/articles/320935

Susan Albers, P. (2021, November 12). Emotional eating: What it is and tips to manage it. Cleveland Clinic. https://health.clevelandclinic.org/emo-tional-eating/

Conner, T. S., DeYoung, C. G., & Silvia, P. J. (2018). Everyday creative activity is a path to flourishing. The Journal of Positive Psychology, 13(2), 181–189. https://doi.org/10.1080/17439760.2016.1257049

Kenley, H. (n.d.). Mountain Air: Relapsing and Finding the Way Back... One breath at a time.

Werner, C., RD, & Dias, A. (ren). (2022, September 2). Emotional eating: Why it happens and how to stop it. Healthline. https://www.healthline.-com/health/emotional-eating

What is binge eating relapse, and reasons why it happens. (2022, October 12). Dr. Nina Inc. https://drninainc.com/dr-nina-show/binge-eating-relapse/

(N.d.). Nationaleatingdisorders.org. https://www.nationaleatingdisorder-s.org/learn/general-information/recovery

NHS. (2021, February 1). 10 stress busters. Nhs. uk. https://www.nhs.uk/mental-health/self-help/guides-tools-and-activi-ties/tips-to-reduce-stress/

Scott, E. (2021, July 29). 17 Highly Effective Stress Relievers. Verywell Mind; Verywellmind. https://www.verywellmind.com/tips-to-reduce-stress-3145195

Hitti, M. (2016, December 13). 10 Tips to Manage Stress. WebMD. https://www.webmd.com/balance/guide/tips-to-control-stress

Jennings, K.-A. (2018, August 28). 16 Simple Ways to Relieve Stress and Anxiety. Healthline. https://www.healthline.com/nutrition/16-ways-relieve-stress-anxiety#The-bottom-line

Stress: 10 Ways To Relieve Stress. (2022, May 26). Cleveland Clinic. https://health.clevelandclinic.org/how-to-relieve-stress/

25 Quick Ways to Reduce Stress. (2014, December 16). Colorado Law. https://www.colorado.edu/law/25-quick-ways-reduce-stress

(Sissons, C. (2019, January 8). L-theanine: Benefits, risks, sources, and dosage. Medicalnewstoday.com. https://www.medicalnewstoday.-com/articles/324120)

(Arslan Khalid, Ahmad Bilal Arif, Wei Wang, Ping Li. (2022). The correlation between procrastination and perceived stress & parenting styles of Chinese medical students. https://doi.org/10.14456/ITJEMAST.2022.78)

6 steps to changing bad eating habits. (n.d.). WebMD. https://www.webmd.-com/diet/obesity/features/6-steps-to-changing-bad-eating-habits

Healthy eating: Changing your eating habits. (n.d.). Kaiserpermanente.orgfrom https://wa.kaiserpermanente.org/kbase/topic.jhtml?docId=ad1169

How to eat slower: 6 strategies. (n.d.). Psychology Today. https://www.psychologytoday.com/us/blog/comfort-cravings/201604/how-eat-slower-6-strategies

Parker-Pope, T. (2022, January 10). Cookies? Chips? Pizza? Here's how to own your cravings. The New York Times. https://www.nytimes.-com/2022/01/10/well/eat/food-cravings-strategies.html

Setting reasonable goals for eating disorders recovery. (2012, May 9). Eating Disorder Hope. https://www.eatingdisorderhope.com/recovery/self-help-tools-skills-tips/goal-setting

Stiefvater, S. (2021, January 19). PureWow. PureWow. https://www.pure-wow.com/wellness/healthy-eating-quotes

The Rule of three: A guide to healthy eating. (n.d.). FitFormula Wellness https://fitformulawellness.com/blogs/blog/the-rule-of-three-a-guide-to-healthy-eating

Eating due to envy or jealousy. (n.d.). Karen R. Koenig - Author https://www.karenrkoenig.com/blog/eating-due-to-envy-or-jealousy

O'Connor, A. (2012, December 6). 10 emotional traps that trigger overeating. Health. https://www.health.com/food/10-emotional-traps-that-trigger-overeating

Garcia, G. D., Pompeo, D. A., Eid, L. P., Cesarino, C. B., Pinto, M. H., & Gonçalves, L. W. P. (2018). Relationship between anxiety, depressive symptoms and compulsive overeating disorder in patients with cardiovascular diseases. Revista Latino-Americana de Enfermagem, 26, e3040. https://doi.org/10.1590/1518-8345.2567.3040

Linardon, J. (2020, June 13). Emotional eating: Why it happens and 5 steps to stop it. Break Binge Eating. https://breakbingeeating.com/emotional-eating/

Pedersen, T. (2022, June 17). Controlling your emotions: Is it possible? Psych Central. https://psychcentral.com/blog/controlling-emotions-is-it-possible

Stanger, M. (2019, November 26). What is the Root of Emotional Eating? Talkspace. https://www.talkspace.com/blog/food-addiction-emotional-eating-root-cause/

Torrence, B. S., & Connelly, S. (2019). Emotion regulation tendencies and leadership performance: An examination of cognitive and behavioral regulation strategies. Frontiers in Psychology, 10, 1486. https://doi.org/10.3389/fpsyg.2019.01486

Van Bockstaele, B., Atticciati, L., Hiekkaranta, A. P., Larsen, H., & Verschuere, B. (2020). Choose change: Situation modification, distraction, and reappraisal in mild versus intense negative situations. Motivation and Emotion, 44(4), 583–596. https://doi.org/10.1007/s11031-019-09811-8

Zhou, A., Xie, P., Tian, Z., & Pan, C. (2021). The influence of emotion on eating behavior. Xin Li Ke Xue Jin Zhan, 29(11), 2013. https://doi.org/10.3724/sp.j.1042.2021.02013

(N.d.-a). Inc.com. https://www.inc.com/justin-bariso/28-emotional-intelligence-quotes-that-can-help-make-emotions-work-for-you-instead-of-against-you.html

(N.d.-b). Psycom.net https://www.psycom.net/emotions-that-trigger-overeating

4 ways to boost your self-compassion. (2021, February 12). Harvard Health. https://www.health.harvard.edu/mental-health/4-ways-to-boost-your-self-compassion

Binge eating quotes. (n.d.). Goodreads.com. https://www.goodreads.com/quotes/tag/binge-eating

Davidson, K., MScFN, RD, & CPT. (2020, December 3). 5 tips for developing a better relationship with food. Healthline. https://www.healthline.com/nutrition/fixing-a-bad-relationship-with-food

Nutrition: Keeping a food diary. (2000, September 1). Familydoctor.org. https://familydoctor.org/nutrition-keeping-a-food-diary/

The Counseling Teacher. (2018, March 19). 5 ways to reframe negative thoughts. Confident Counselors. https://confidentcounselors.com/2018/03/19/reframe-negative-thoughts/

Top 10 ways to DE-stress and eat less. (n.d.). WebMD. https://www.webmd.com/mental-health/features/top-10-ways-to-destress-and-eat-less

Website, N. H. S. (n.d.). 10 stress busters. Nhs.uk. https://www.nhs.uk/mental-health/self-help/guides-tools-and-activities/tips-to-reduce-stress/

Weight loss. (2020, December 9). Mayo Clinic. https://www.mayoclinic.org/healthy-lifestyle/weight-loss/in-depth/weight-loss/art-20047342

Binge Eating Disorder - health risks and complications. (2017, January 18).

Walden Eating Disorders; Walden Behavioral Care. https://www.waldeneatingdisorders.com/what-we-treat/binge-eating-disorder/binge-eating-disorder-health-risks/

Binge eating disorder and mindfulness/DBT. (2017, August 30). Eating Disorder Hope. https://www.eatingdisorderhope.com/information/binge-eating-disorder/binge-eating-disorder-and-mindfulnessdbt

Binge eating disorder health risks. (n.d.). Eating Recovery Center. https://www.eatingrecoverycenter.com/conditions/binge-eating/health-risks

Faculty By Department, & Find a Physician. (n.d.). Understanding compulsive overeating. Rochester.edu. https://www.urmc.rochester.edu/encyclopedia/content.aspx?contenttypeid=56&contentid=4132

Understanding compulsive eating disorder: Symptoms, causes, & treatment. (2021, August 14). Eating Disorder Hope. https://www.eatingdisorderhope.com/compulsive-overeating-disorder

Uotani, S. (2019, January 10). How to overcome emotional eating using mindfulness meditation. Better Humans. https://betterhumans.pub/how-to-use-mindfulness-meditation-to-overcome-emotional-eating-aa95003cfe64

Brown, N. (2020, August 1). Why food can't make you happy. It Begins With A Thought Coaching; It Begins With a Thought. https://itbeginswithathought.com/why-food-cant-make-you-happy/

Byrne, C. (2021, July 1). Why you're obsessed with food — and how to stop it. Christine Byrne; Christine Byrne, MPH, RD, LDN. https://christinejbyrne.com/why-youre-obsessed-with-food-and-how-to-stop/

Dror, C. (2020, June 23). 5 unexpected causes of your intense food cravings. Camille Styles. https://camillestyles.com/wellness/5-unexpected-causes-intense-food-cravings/

People Skills. (2011, December 23). 12 signs of emotional eating (and why it is bad for you). Personal Excellence. https://personalexcellence.co/blog/signs-of-emotional-eating/

Rumsey, A. (2021, December 20). How to stop eating when full & find comfortable fullness. Alissa Rumsey. https://alissarumsey.com/how-to-stop-eating-when-full/

Sinusoid, D. (2021, November 1). Positive feedback loop: The psychology of habit formation. Shortform Books. https://www.shortform.com/blog/positive-feedback-loop-psychology/

Treleaven, S. (2013, May 28). How happiness can trigger overeating. Chatelaine. https://www.chatelaine.com/health/how-happiness-can-trigger-overeating/

Werner, C., RD, & Dias, A. (ren). (2022, September 2). Emotional eating:

Why it happens and how to stop it. Healthline. https://www.healthline.com/health/emotional-eating

What is comfort food and why is it so comforting. (2021, January 21). The Nuttery. https://thenutteryny.com/blog/what-is-comfort-food.html

Why stress causes people to overeat. (2021, February 15). Harvard Health. https://www.health.harvard.edu/staying-healthy/why-stress-causes-people-to-overeat

Dodier, S. (2017, April 13). 5 signs of emotional eating: Are you an emotional eater? Thrive Global. https://medium.com/thrive-global/5-signs-of-emotional-eating-are-you-an-emotional-eater-d7fc6obaf668

Emotional eating - Helpguide.org. (n.d.). https://www.helpguide.org/articles/diets/emotional-eating.htm

Emotional eating - HelpGuide.Org. (n.d.). https://www.helpguide.org/articles/diets/emotional-eating.htm

Why stress causes people to overeat. (2021, February 15). Harvard Health. https://www.health.harvard.edu/staying-healthy/why-stress-causes-people-to-overeat

Ducharme, J. (2018, July 31). Here's Why You Stress Eat — And How to Stop Doing It. Time. https://time.com/5347612/how-to-stop-stress-eating/

Werner, C., RD, & Dias, A. (ren). (2022, September 2). Emotional Eating: Why It Happens and How to Stop It. Healthline. https://www.healthline.com/health/emotional-eating

Yau, Y. H. C., & Potenza, M. N. (2013). Stress and eating behaviors. Minerva Endocrinologica, 38(3), 255–267.

Scott, E. (n.d.). Why You Binge Eat When You're Not Hungry. Verywell Mind. https://www.verywellmind.com/what-causes-emotional-eating-or-stress-eating-3145261

Binge eating and pregnancy. (n.d.). WebMD. https://www.webmd.com/mental-health/eating-disorders/binge-eating-disorder/binge-eating-pregnancy

Eddins, R. (n.d.). Why emotional eating can be a consequence of trauma. PACEsConnection. https://www.pacesconnection.com/blog/why-emotional-eating-can-be-a-consequence-of-trauma

Ducharme, J. (2018, July 31). Here's why you stress eat — and how to stop doing it. Time. https://time.com/5347612/how-to-stop-stress-eating/

Emotional eating - Helpguide.org. (n.d.). https://www.helpguide.org/articles/diets/emotional-eating.htm

Emotional Eating Quotes. (n.d.). Goodreads.com. https://www.goodreads.com/quotes/tag/emotional-eating

Gasbarre, K. (2022, April 18). 5 ways stress-eating impacts your gut health, mood, and more, say eating psychology specialists. The Healthy. https://www.thehealthy.com/mental-health/stress-eating-effects/

Lindberg, S. (2021, January 20). Why do I eat when I'm stressed? Healthline. https://www.healthline.com/health/healthy-eating/why-do-i-eat-when-im-stressed

Nicole Galan, R. N. (2018, February 15). Emotional eating: How to overcome stress eating. Medicalnewstoday.com. https://www.medicalnewstoday.com/articles/320935

Stress eating: What is it and how do you stop it? (n.d.). Ro. https://ro.co/health-guide/stress-eating/

Susan Albers, P. (2021, November 12). Emotional eating: What it is and tips to manage it. Cleveland Clinic. https://health.clevelandclinic.org/emotional-eating/

The Effects of emotional eating. (2018, March 29). LiveWell Dorset. https://www.livewelldorset.co.uk/articles/the-effects-of-emotional-eating/

(N.d.-a). Harvard.edu. https://www.health.harvard.edu/staying-healthy/why-stress-causes-people-to-overeat

(N.d.-b). Harvard.edu. https://www.health.harvard.edu/staying-healthy/why-stress-causes-people-to-overeat#:~:text=Stress%20eating%2C%20hormones%20and%20hunger&text=High%20cortisol%20levels%2C%20in%20combination,stress%20related%20responses%20and%20emotic

Epel, E., Lapidus, R., McEwen, B., & Brownell, K. (2001). Stress may add bite to appetite in women: a laboratory study of stress-induced cortisol and eating behavior. Psychoneuroendocrinology, 26(1), 37–49. https://doi.org/10.1016/s0306-4530(00)00035-4

(N.d.-a). Nih.gov. https://www.ncbi.nlm.nih.gov/pubmed/?term=Morning+and+afternoon+appetite+and+gut+hormone+responses+to+meal+and+stress

(N.d.-b). Apa.org. https://www.apa.org/news/press/releases/stress/2017/state-nation.pdf

Printed in Great Britain
by Amazon

25276032R00086